Around the Spanish Main

HUGH O'SHAUGHNESSY

Around
the Spanish Main

Travels in the Caribbean
and the Guianas

CENTURY
LONDON SYDNEY AUCKLAND JOHANNESBURG

To Hugo with love

First published in Great Britain in 1991 by
Century
Random Century House
20 Vauxhall Bridge Road, London SW1V 2SA

A catalogue record for this book is available from
the British Library

ISBN 0 7126 3807 5

Typeset in Imprint by SX Composing Ltd
Printed and bound in Great Britain by
Mackays of Chatham

Contents

*Photographs by Hugh O'Shaughnessy
appear between pp. 90-91*

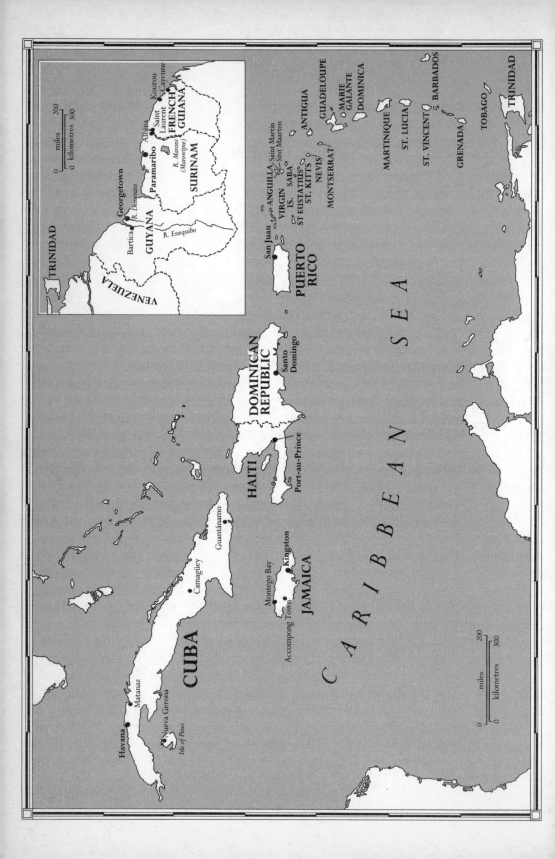

Introduction

'The whites are there as units among hundreds, and the
proportion cannot be altered.'

James Anthony Froude, *The English in the West Indies*.

'Considering that slavery in the United States did not
end until 1865, it is no wonder that the West Indian
negro today is a much more relaxed, urbane and socially
adjusted creature than his counterpart in America. He
had a start of twenty-seven years over his American
brother in the enjoyment of full civil rights. Added to
this is the very important factor that whereas in America
the black men constituted a minority group – and still do
– the white men in the Caribbean were, and still are, in
the minority.'

Edgar Mittelholzer, *With a Carib Eye*.

I had never experienced such sun, at the same time burning,
oppressive, intrusive and caressing. Used to the showers
and drizzle of northern Europe, I marvelled at the wide gut-
ters that the streets of Port of Spain needed to drain the water
from tropical storms. Equally, I was amazed once to be sitting in
a Land Rover and not to be able to see to the front of the vehicle's very short bonnet because of the intensity of the downpour.
Used to nothing more exotic in the plant world than the contents
of the carefully tended hothouses of Kew Gardens, across the
Thames from the house in which I grew up, I was amazed at the
restless spontaneity of the vegetation of Trinidad that seemed to

grow in front of my eyes.

My visit to the Caribbean in 1962 gave me my first experience of the New World and my first exposure to the *dolce far niente* of the West Indies. The tropical heat, the rain and the strange, wild vegetation, the languor and the gaiety were overpowering and they left an indelible mark on the memory of a young journalist. I had flown out to the Caribbean knowing I would find a culture that was at once African, Indian and European. But, not having seen many West Indians yet on the streets of London, I had naively thought that they had a great deal of European blood in their veins and would all be coffee-coloured. The blackness of the majority of the inhabitants of Trinidad came as a great surprise to me.

I was to go to the Caribbean on countless other occasions, visiting countries and islands where they spoke Spanish, French and Dutch, the places familiar to outsiders, like Barbados and Puerto Rico and the less well-known territories such as Surinam and Anegada.

Shortly after the missile crisis of 1962 I went to report on Cuba. The mass suicide of the devotees of the mad Jim Jones took me to Guyana in 1978 and the US invasion of Grenada to that island in 1983. Prime Minister George Price invited me to Belize for the ceremonies in 1981 when his country became independent of Britain. I looked at the damage done to Jamaica after Hurricane Gilbert in 1988 and to Guadeloupe by Hurricane Hugo the following year. The attempted coup of Abu Bakr meant another visit to Trinidad in 1990.

The newspapers for which I worked provided me with a particularly intensive course in Caribbean affairs, often sending me to report on islands which were seldom in the news.

This book is in part an attempt to convey to readers who are not familiar with the region – and indeed to some who are – something of the physical beauty, the historical interest, the human friendships and the occasional political revulsion that I experienced in various journeys to the islands and to the Guianas. Many places are left out; the book has no pretensions to being geographically exhaustive.

My other aim is to take up the hopeful words which were written in 1958 in the era of colonialism by the Guyanese writer Edgar Mittelholzer which I cite above. They were true when they were written and are even more true now that many parts of the region have emerged from colonialism and their optimistic message is, I feel, not sufficiently heeded.

The peoples of the Caribbean have recovered amazingly quickly from their history, the first massacres and the criminal regime of slavery on which present societies were founded in the seventeenth and eighteenth centuries.

The shaping of the modern Caribbean started with the haphazard genocide carried out by the first Spaniards against the Indians. The Tainos, the inhabitants of Hispaniola, today occupied by Haïti and the Dominican Republic, numbered about 600,000 when Columbus discovered the New World in 1492. They were put to work by the Spaniards digging for the small quantities of gold there were on the island. A census in 1508 showed that nine out of ten of them had died! The culture shock of being forced into slavery from one day to the next by an alien people was too much for them. Abortion became widespread and many adults killed their children and poisoned themselves with the juice of the yellow yucca.

The first recorded protest against the Spaniards' treatment of native peoples came on the Sunday before Christmas in 1511 when a Dominican friar, Antonio de Montesinos, preached in Santo Domingo.

'In order,' he said, 'to make your sins against the Indians known to you I have come up on this pulpit, I who am a voice of Christ crying in the wilderness of this island, and therefore it behooves you to listen, not with careless attention, but with all your heart and senses, so that you may hear it; for this is going to be the strangest that ever you expected to hear . . . This voice says that you are in mortal sin, that you live and die in it, for the cruelty and tyranny you use in dealing with these innocent people. Tell me, by what right or justice do you keep these Indians in such a cruel and horrible servitude? On what authority have you waged a detestable war against these people, who dwelt quietly and peacefully in their own land? . . . Why do you keep them so oppressed and weary, not giving them enough to eat nor taking care of them in their illness? For with the excessive work you demand of them they fall ill and die, or rather you kill them with your desire to extract and acquire gold every day. And what care do you take that they should be instructed in religion? . . . Are these not men? Have they not rational souls? Are you not bound to love them as you love yourselves?'

His congregation did not mend its ways, indeed the local Spaniards were indignant. By 1517 there were only 11,000 Tainos left on the island, ruled over by 700 Spaniards. The following year there was an epidemic of smallpox which reduced their numbers to 3,000; by 1550 there were no survivors. The Taino culture had been completely erased by the European influence.

The state of affairs in Hispaniola was soon replicated throughout the hemisphere with the terrible slave economies instituted by every ruling white power from the British to the Danes.

The horrors of the killing of the first peoples of America and of the trade in slaves who had to be brought in from Africa to replace them have been well and extensively studied and described by scholars. Out of every hundred men, women and children who were shipped out of West Africa or the Congo to be slaves, fifteen on average died on the terrible, overcrowded transatlantic voyage, their corpses being thrown over the side. Once in the Caribbean, as we shall see, they were set to a working life of cruelty and abuse.

It took more than three centuries for any decisive action to be taken on Montesinos' appeal. In Britain, the figure of William Wilberforce who helped the emancipation process is rightly honoured. The evangelical MP for Hull, a rich man with excellent connections with the highest in the land, started a campaign in the House of Commons in 1789. Because of his, and others', efforts the trade in slaves was abolished in 1807. In 1823 he helped to found the Anti-Slavery Society. Finally in August 1833, a month after his death, the Emancipation Bill was passed at Westminster. He was recognised as one of the most influential men of his day and buried with suitable respect in Westminster Abbey.

Wilberforce and others who worked with him are well remembered: more dimly remembered are the thousands of British traders who made large quantities of money in this repellent trade and who created English prosperity in Bristol and

Liverpool and other ports and cities.

Slave trading was a crime which involved virtually every country in Europe. Nantes and Bordeaux were the French counterparts of Bristol and Liverpool, and some part of the prosperity of cities from Cadiz to Amsterdam (the Dutch did not abolish slavery in their territories until 1863), Copenhagen and even Riga was due to the riches resulting from the Caribbean slave trade.

In France, Victor Schoelcher is revered as the apostle of the emancipation of French slaves. The law he had passed in 1848 compelled the freeing of the slaves which had been declared with revolutionary fervour in 1794 but was never put into force. The former porcelain salesman gave up a good job in his father's business after he had visited the Western hemisphere and seen slavery at first hand. He then devoted years to collecting evidence about slavery worldwide. Together with Alphonse de Lamartine and Victor Hugo, and with help from the abolitionists in Britain, he lobbied long and hard in Paris for the end of slavery. In the French West Indies there is not a town or a village without a street named after Schoelcher, and a bust erected to his memory looks down on you from a plinth in every square.

It is strange that the atrocity of slavery seems to weigh more lightly on the conscience of the Western world than other, later crimes. Perhaps the series of killings in two world wars have dulled our sensitivities.

The Jews have rightly and understandably documented the terrible harm inflicted on their communities in twentieth-century Europe. Sadly, of the million of blacks who died on board ship as they were being taken from Africa or who worked in the plantations of the New World, there are no such accurate records. Family history for most blacks in the Western hemisphere is a riddle which is never going to be solved. As the Jamaican poet Olive Senior wrote in *Cockpit Country Dreams*,

'. . . Undocumented
I drown in the other's history.'

It is no wonder that the themes of lost identity and new identity are constant ones in the West Indies. (I am conscious, too, that it is the reason why all too many of the historical references in this book are to the activities of the European minority rather than to the majorities of blacks, of African descent, or East Indians, whose forefathers migrated from the Indian subcontinent.)

Given such a context it is little short of miraculous how many territories, among the states of the English-speaking Caribbean at least, have emerged in the late twentieth century as generally tolerant, multi-racial societies.

In *The English in the West Indies* in 1888, James Anthony Froude took a dismal view of the future of the area. An influential British historian of his generation, he harked back to a former age in the Caribbean when, 'The white settlers ruled as in Ireland, the slaves obeyed, and all went swimmingly.' He forecast gloomily that Whitehall's unwillingness to support the former slave owners and to crack the imperial whip in the Caribbean would be fatal.

He wrote, 'force on them black parliamentary institutions . . . and these beautiful countries will become like Hayti, with Obeah triumphant, and children offered to the devil and salted and eaten, till the conscience of mankind wakes again and the Americans sweep them all away. Home Rule for the West Indies would transform them into "so many fresh Irelands".'

Obeah, in the form of voodoo, is certainly alive in Haïti; it was one of the instruments of government of the late President-for-Life François Duvalier. It must be noted, however, that 'the conscience of mankind' did not wake in time and the Americans, otherwise so active in the Caribbean, did not sweep his dictatorship away. The tyrant died in his bed unmolested by any Western government: his son Jean-Claude was gently flown by the French government to a life of gilded exile in Europe.

Moreover a century later all thirteen of Britain's former Caribbean colonies which have now achieved independence have avoided the horror predicted by Froude. Under black parliamentary institutions they are certainly more at peace than Northern Ireland is under white parliamentary institutions.

The dark shadow of extreme racialism scarred Caribbean societies for generations after the slaves were set free. In 1966 Jean Rhys, the gifted white writer from Dominica, set out in her novel, *The Wide Sargasso Sea*, the horrors of the murderous antagonisms she knew existed between black and white people and which so haunted her.

Yet by 1991 a great deal of the most bitter racial antagonism has blown away. Race relations are far from perfect not only between black and white but also, in Trinidad and Guyana, between negro and East Indian. Yet they are far better than anyone might have hoped in colonial times, and are certainly at the other end of the spectrum from the situation in South Africa.

In most parts of the Caribbean there are societies which are ruled over by politicians who work a parliamentary system, who take account of the opinions of the majorities, yet do not seek to repress their minorities.

The new states certainly have their problems. There are blemishes on the political faces of many territories in the form of corruption, incompetence, small-mindedness. As states which are among the world's smallest, they are economically fragile, vulnerable to the smallest fall in the international price of their exports of bananas, coffee or bauxite and, in the last instance, dependent on the goodwill of the world's largest economies.

On my first visit to Trinidad the political facts about the West Indies did not impress me as forcefully as did the climate and the vegetation. Though I did not realize it fully at the time, a decent society was emerging into independence as I landed there. Trinidad in 1962 was a colony on the eve of achieving an easy separation from Britain and was living in a colonial twilight. There was a British governor and a force of colonial police and such pillars of the colonial establishment as the *Trinidad Guardian* newspaper and Barclays Bank Dominion Colonial and Overseas. But there was also expectation in the air among the Trinidadians. Among the expatriate businessmen, many of whom still echoed the views of Froude, there was some foreboding about the political future of the island under the leadership of the Oxford scholar and intellectual giant Eric Williams. Williams, who while Trinidad and Tobago was still a colony enjoyed the title of 'premier', was to become the prime minister of an independent Trinidad and Tobago later that year. The classes in politics that he delivered to the crowds who came to hear him talk under the trees of 'The University of Woodford Square' in the centre of Port of Spain had moulded the political thinking of Trinidadians. The oil company executives whom I talked to whispered about how he would find it difficult to avoid racial tensions between Africans and East Indians on the island and about how he

7

had once flirted with communism and might well do so again.

Trinidad and Tobago has now been independent for nearly thirty years. The country has gone through an oil boom and a subsequent depression but it has also acquired a good deal of self-assurance. Eric Williams is dead and, tragically, in the years immediately before his death he had become estranged from his people. But the People's National Movement which he had founded is still alive. Though there is some distrust still between the Africans and the East Indians in Trinidad there is nothing approaching the sort of crisis that Idi Amin provoked with the Asians in Uganda or that exists between Tamils and Sinhalese in Sri Lanka. In the functioning parliamentary regime Williams established, fair elections now take place, and power passed peacefully from the PNM to the opposition National Alliance for Reconstruction after the elections in 1986.

The failed attempt at a *putsch* by Yasin Abu Bakr, the naive leader of a small 'black Muslim' group in Port of Spain in July 1990 caused great damage and lamentation in Trinidad. But everything points to the fact that the country's parliamentary regime derived strength from the traumas precisely because most Trinidadians, however discontent they were with their elected government, were not prepared to see it overthrown by force, much less by the forces of tiny and unrepresentative minorities.

There are many places in the Caribbean which have a record similar to that of Trinidad. The government in Barbados has alternated between the Barbados Labour Party and the Democratic Labour Party – whose policies are extremely difficult for non-Barbadians to tell apart – with great regularity after clean elections and in total calm. St Lucia has experienced a more complicated and tortuous political history but has preserved a parliamentary system with two main parties.

After independence in 1978 Dominica experienced a period during which financial scandal, attempted coups and general uncertainty were the norm. Several lives were lost. The island acquired its own conservative Iron Lady in the person of Eugenia Charles, a firm supporter of the invasion of Grenada. In 1987 the government of the United States presented her with the James Monroe award, named after the president who in 1823 propounded the Monroe Doctrine, the founding document of

Washington's pretensions to hegemony in the Western hemisphere.

Power has passed constitutionally from government to opposition in St Kitts and Nevis, the old trade-union based St Kitts Labour Party giving way to the more business-oriented People's Action Movement of Dr Kennedy Simmonds. The recent history of St Vincent has been similar with the conservative James Mitchell and his New Democratic Party ousting the old Milton Cato and the St Vincent Labour Party.

On the mainland of Central America in 1984 the Belizean electorate voted to end a thirty-four-year period of rule by the People's United Party and its leader George Price and opted for a period of more conservative rule with the United Democratic Party. They have since gone back peacefully to preferring the PUP again. In that underpopulated country parliamentary politics have survived the strains which arose from an influx of refugees from the violence of its Spanish-speaking neighbours.

Elections have certainly brought violence and death in Jamaica, the country of the Commonwealth Caribbean where the wounds inflicted by Europe's slave-trading are not yet fully healed, and where the gap between rich and poor is most marked. In the 1980 election about 600 people were killed in battles between the two main parties, the Jamaica Labour Party on the right and the social democratic People's National Party on the left. When the PNP boycotted the elections of 1983 it seemed as though Jamaican society was on the verge of breaking up into chaos. It has not yet happened and power has been transferred back and forth between the parties without *coup d'état* or revolution.

To say this is not to ignore the problems faced by Caribbean societies or the occasions when they have fallen away from high standards of civilized behaviour. Their economies, as I have said, are fragile; their political systems are constantly undermined by the trade in cocaine and marijuana which flows across them catering for the drug addicts of much wealthier countries; they have been in danger of attack by their larger neighbours; there is not enough work for the population; many are forced to emigrate if they want to better themselves.

Unlike the British who gave political independence to their former colonies, the French opted to try and make their

Caribbean territories integral parts of the French republic. Guadeloupe, Martinique and Cayenne are as much *départements* of
France as are the Var, Bouches-du-Rhône or Landes. At great
cost to the French treasury, this integrationist policy has lifted
the standard of living for many in the territories far above the
average in the independent countries of the region. It has meant
that half the salaries paid are government salaries and it has
helped the three *départements* to import seven times more goods
than they export. But though the regime has brought some material prosperity it has not brought political peace or finally solved
the colonial question. Blacks feel they still have to emigrate to
metropolitan France if they want to improve their lot and some
of those who stay are resentful of the freedom with which white
French citizens can settle in the sun on their islands. The French
territories are prosperous and generally peaceful but calls, sometimes violent calls, for independence are still heard.

The Dutch have, much to their regret, not been able to cut
free of all their Caribbean possessions. Surinam became independent in 1975 and before long collapsed into chaos. The other
five and a half Dutch islands, tiny, reasonably prosperous, self-
governing communities with minute populations, quarrel and
feud among themselves with all the parochialism the Caribbean
can muster. They seem to conspire to cause The Hague the same
sort of embarrassment that the few thousand inhabitants of
Anguilla caused Britain when they seceded from St Kitts and
Nevis in 1969 and their island had to be invaded by a force sent
from Britain. The politics of the Dutch Antilles are those of Ruritania in the sun.

There is little good to be said about some of the regimes. The
political situation in the Spanish-speaking Caribbean has fallen
well short of the political sophistication of much of the English-
speaking Caribbean. Haïti is still a political football, suffering its
own racial division between blacks and mulattos. It is, too, the
plaything of outside governments which seem unable to forgive
the Haïtians for their impudence in becoming the first black republic in the world two centuries ago. In the English-speaking
Caribbean the People's National Congress in Guyana has been in
power illegitimately for all too long. Such regimes, however, are
in the minority.

No Caribbean society – not even Surinam under its military

dictatorship – has sunk to the degree of violence which produced the tens of thousands of deaths in El Salvador in the 1980s.

In very few places in the Commonwealth Caribbean are inhabitants deprived of their electoral rights, subjected to death, torture or to the censorship of their reading matter as was the case for many years in certain parts of supposedly more advanced Latin America.

Central America has produced scores of political monsters – Duarte, Cristiani and d'Aubuisson in El Salvador, the Somozas in Nicaragua, Trujillo in the Dominican Republic, Ríos Montt in Guatemala, to name but some of the most recent – the hands of each of whom were stained with the blood of thousands of innocents.

No such monsters have gained power in the English-speaking Caribbean countries.

Sir Eric Gairy of Grenada, some have argued, had the psychological make-up to become a political monster of a type similar to Argentina's Videla or Chile's Pinochet. But even the number of Gairy's political victims seems paltry compared with those of the mildest of the Latin American dictators.

While tens of thousands have fled the rule of the People's National Congress in Guyana the list of political murders carried out by the regime in that country is a sad but nevertheless short one. It hardly extends farther than Walter Rodney and Bernard Darke, the scholar and the Jesuit who were killed by pro-government thugs in Georgetown.

Where there is misrule in the Caribbean this is the responsibility usually of rascals, sometimes of villains, but almost never of the sort of monsters who are to be found on the American mainland.

The suffering of millions who for three centuries were wrenched from their native lands, religion and cultures in Africa, crowded to suffocation into slave ships and put to servitude in the fields and factories of the New World has not been in vain. Nor has the suffering been fruitless for those who in the nineteenth century came, apparently with greater freedom, from India, China, Madeira and elsewhere to supply the labour which after the abolition of the slave trade no longer came from Africa. (These indentured labourers may not have arrived manacled and shackled like the Africans, but the economic pressures which

11

persuaded them to quit their homes can scarcely have been much less compelling than the physical coercion exercised in earlier years by the slave masters on the Africans.) The descendants of the Africans have grown up shielded from the tribalism which has produced such hopeless division and warfare in Africa; among the East Indians the Hindus have been spared the extremes of the caste system as it is practised in modern India while the Muslims, with the exception of such as the small group in Trinidad, have lived in peace with people of other religions. And these uprooted people, whether African or Asian, have had the wisdom to embrace many of the best elements they found in the European societies that enslaved them and to reject the worst.

Despite their comparative poverty these societies have produced not only generally decent government but also music, dance and other art forms which have appealed to tens of millions. Without the work of the Haïtian primitive painters, Jamaican musicians like Bob Marley, Cuban Bands like Los Van Van, Trinidadian calypsonians like Mighty Sparrow, the writings of Aimé Césaire of Guadeloupe, Derek Walcott of St Lucia, Edward Kamau Brathwaite of Barbados, or Caryl Phillips of St Kitts, to say nothing of cricketers, boxers and athletes, the world would be a poorer place.

All too little credit, I feel, is given by the world to these Caribbean societies. And indeed they themselves are too slow in claiming it. Slavery, it has often been said, did more than take away the liberty of those who were enslaved: it took away their self-respect. The recovery of that self-respect has been a painful process, full of contradictions.

From the first days of enforced labour the slaves longed to return to their origins, the source of their self-respect. But as the African-born generations died out, first-hand memories of Africa were effaced. These memories gave way to other ways of maintaining self-respect. First-hand memory of Benin or of Biafra was superseded by a naïve and undifferentiated longing for 'Africa', a longing which made little distinction between Ibos and Yorubas, the Nile or the Zambezi, Zimbabwe or Dahomey.

In Jamaica – and it must be no accident that it happened in a country where the memory of slavery is still vivid – this longing helped the emergence of Rastafarianism. The cult emerged in

1930, the year in which Ras Tafari, who had ruled Ethiopia successively as regent and king, had himself crowned emperor as Haile Selassie in Addis Ababa.

The new emperor, an energetic reformer when he came to power, was seized on in Jamaica as the reincarnation of Christ and as the man capable of leading blacks out of bondage in the Jamaican Babylon and back to their African homeland in Ethiopia. His country after all had a long recorded history and a Christian church which was fifteen centuries old. It had defeated an Italian army of 13,000 at Adowa in 1896, routing the colonialism of Rome, and it would help to defeat Mussolini in the Second World War.

The emperor made a tumultuously popular visit to Kingston in 1966 when there were moves to have him replace Elizabeth II as Jamaica's Head of State. Rastafarianism has survived Haile Selassie's denial of his own divinity, and his overthrow and death. Marihuana is still its sacred weed and the green, yellow and red colours of the Ethiopian flag are seen still on rings worn on a million black fingers, and some white ones. Rastafarianism has taken its place beside Mormonism, for example, as another of the fantastical millenarian doctrines which bewildered men in America have invented to comfort themselves in a lonely New World.

The longing which produced the Rasta faith had already moved Marcus Garvey, also a Jamaican. In the 1920s he persuaded six million blacks in the United States to nominate a 'provisional government for Africa' and plan the return of the members of his Universal Negro Improvement Association *en masse* to the continent. Garvey was nominated His Highness the Potentate, Provisional President of Africa. His more prominent helpers became Knight of the Nile, Baron Zambesi, Viscount of the Niger or Earl of the Congo, with rather less presumption than do the Mormon leaders in Salt Lake City who style themselves Apostles to this day. Garvey was certainly the victim of delusions but the example of his life's work transcended these delusions. He summed up his greater aims when he declared,

'I shall teach the black man to see beauty in himself.'

He is rightly looked upon by Rastafarians as a prophet of their faith and in 1965 he was named by the government Jamaica's first National Hero.

The nobler strands in Garvey's thought or in the activities of the Rastas have not always been understood or welcomed by West Indian intellectuals. One of the best known West Indian writers, the Trinidadian, Vidia Naipaul, for instance, has devoted many pages in his early novels to scoffing at the West Indies. Despite his great literary gifts he was slow to appreciate the gradual recovery of black self-respect or the emergence of tolerant multi-racial arrangements in which people of East Indian descent like himself lived harmoniously with blacks after the colonial master had gone. In his novel, *The Mimic Men*, he made easy fun by ridiculing the identity problems of his compatriots and the empty pretensions they often affected.

In his book, *The Middle Passage*, for instance, Naipaul wrote that he knew on his return to Trinidad after a spell living in London that the island was 'unimportant, uncreative, cynical'. Despite being a master of English prose and being able to puncture the false and pretentious in West Indian society unerringly he showed little awareness of the civic strengths and virtues that were emerging in his native country.

More radical figures than Naipaul also display a reluctance to appreciate the qualities of their own societies. Sitting in the house of an Antiguan politician with an honorable record of opposition to apartheid, I was surprised to hear him wonder miserably what sort of lesson newly enfranchised blacks in South Africa could learn from the Caribbean, if any. Only with difficulty would he accept my critical admiration of the tolerant nature of the Caribbean way of life.

If this book, as it tells of journeys in the Caribbean, also draws some attention to those many aspects of Caribbean society which other people in many other parts of the world should envy it will achieve its aim.

Chapter One

The Middle Passage

'The stench of the hold, while we were on the coast, was so intolerably loathsome, that it was dangerous to remain there for any time, and some of us had been permitted to stay on the deck for the fresh air, but now that the whole ship's cargo were confined together it became absolutely pestilential. The closeness of the place, and the heat of the climate, added to the number in the ship, being so crowded that each had scarcely room to turn himself, almost suffocated us. This produced copious perspiration, so that the air soon became unfit for respiration, from a variety of loathsome smells, and brought on a sickness among the slaves, of which many died, thus falling victims to the improvident avarice, as I may call it, of their purchasers. This deplorable situation was again aggravated by the galling of the chains, now become insupportable; and the filth of necessary tubs, into which the children often fell, and were almost suffocated. The shrieks of the women, and the groans of the dying, rendered it a scene of horror almost inconceivable.'

The Interesting Narrative of the Life of Olaudah Equiano or Gustavus Vassa the African, written by himself.

This is where it all started.

The Slave Coast of West Africa is a beautiful place today. The rollers pound rhythmically on to the broad strand from God knows what watery wilderness in the South Atlantic. The fishermen have built their huts with walls made out of the plaited fronds of the towering palm trees which line the shore. They leave their boats beached upside down on the sand. They pull their catches out of the sea and sell them to the passers-by and they seem to have found the secret of the simple life. They enjoy throughout the year and for nothing what thousands of holiday makers from richer countries pay dearly to enjoy for a fortnight.

Just above the high water mark there stands a large concrete cross put there impudently to commemorate the arrival of some nineteenth-century European missionaries. The Africans have put up no monument to commemorate the hundreds of thousands of their anonymous compatriots, men, women and children who were shipped away from this beach to die on the terrible journey to America or to be worked to the brink of death or beyond it in the New World.

The wounds of history appear to have scarred over. The slave ships which used to ride at anchor and which took Olaudah Equiano and his compatriots to America are no more than the most distant memory. The terrible trade in human bodies and in misery, though not forgotten on the Slave Coast, seems to have been forgiven. Or perhaps it is just that there is no alternative to accepting what has gone before.

Whydah, set a few miles inland across a sluggish lagoon where villagers paddle their dugouts, was once the emporium of slavery where French, British, Portuguese, Danes and Dutch came to bargain with the King of Dahomey for the human beings he wanted to sell. Now it is a quiet decaying town in what was for years a primitive African military dictatorship.

The Slave Coast, once known as Dahomey and now fulsomely and misleadingly called the Popular Republic of Benin, is not in any but the most formal and empty sense a country.

For years the dictator of Benin ruled by a combination of authoritarianism and extreme corruption which smothered any initiative and choked any enterprise. At one point the banks failed and anyone who wanted to do banking business had to cross Benin's eastern frontier into Nigeria or go west into Togo. This man, who name is of no importance, was, moreover, politically schizophrenic. A poster at the airport welcomed the few tourists to 'Benin, the cradle of voodoo': across the main avenue from the airport hung a banner which proclaimed, 'Socialism is our goal: Marxism-Leninism is our path'.

16

Benin is not just an African version of those many primitive dictatorships which have held sway in Latin America. Most of them had some rudimentary sense of national unity. Benin is worse off: it is little more than a starving expanse of West Africa whose frontiers were marked out by Europeans a century ago and whose 4,500,000 inhabitants, plundered and impoverished by their own rulers and by the Europeans alike, have very little in common. Some worship Christ, some revere Mahomet, some adore serpents. There is little sense of nationhood. The broken-down radio service is obliged to carry programmes in French, Yoruba, Hausa, Yom, Dendi, Waama, Biali, Anufom, and a dozen other languages if it is to be understood within Benin's borders.

Little wonder that many people in Benin gave the impression of being bemused, listless and despairing.

'This Monsieur Major, tell me about him.'

My guide in Benin was Thiam Baba Moussa, an eighteen-year-old of amazing quick intelligence and great dignity and self-possession, neither bemused, listless nor despairing. I gave him my view of Monsieur Major.

'And do you think that the new prime minister of New Zealand will be successful?'

I confessed to the enquiring teenager that I was not as familiar with Antipodean politics as he clearly was.

By listening religiously every day to the news broadcasts he could capture on his transistor radio, and by reading whatever foreign newspapers he could lay his hands upon, Thiam had built up an encyclopedic knowledge of the outside world and its politics. To tell the truth, he had little else to do. His school, the Lycée Toffa 1er, had been shut for six months, its gates padlocked, its classrooms cobwebbed and dusty and its basket-ball court deserted. The dictatorship said the closure was because of the teachers' strike. The teachers said it was because corruption and mismanagement had meant that there was nothing left to pay them with. In any event Thiam had lost a year's study and had been robbed of the possession of a *bacca-lauréat*. As the son of the first wife of a Moslem scholar who had made the pilgrimage to Mecca and had translated the *Koran* into one of the local languages Thiam felt the lack of education even more painfully than any other young man of his intelligence.

'All my teachers are taxi drivers now,' Thiam remarked bitterly. This meant they spent their day riding motorbikes. Benin is too poor for four-wheel taxis and passengers have to know how to ride pillion. In a richer country Thiam would have been assured of a dazzling career but it was difficult to see what sort of future indigent, disorganized, dictatorial Benin could offer him.

Thiam's Moslem family was from the north of the country. In Whydah, to judge by the many different places of worship, different religions were competing for the souls of the inhabitants as robustly as the traders had once competed for human bodies in the slave markets. Concrete European saints, some missing an arm, others a head, peered from the whitewashed façade of the large Catholic church, an ugly nineteenth-century pastiche of Burgundian gothic. A more modern mosque bore witness to Muslim proselytism. The most ancient shrine and the only one in Whydah which looked genuinely African was a small, dusty, tree-shaded, walled compound containing hutches made of chicken wire. There dwelt the sacred pythons which the Africans had worshipped for centuries.

The doors of some of the less rickety houses along the sandy, unpaved streets of Whydah bear the names of their owners, Souza, Almeida, dos Santos, reminders of the lingering presence of families from Portugal or of the handful of families of freed slaves who made money in Brazil and who could afford to come home.

'Money, money, money. *Un cadeau*. Gi' me money.'

The tiny children outside the dusty compound which formed the temple of the sacred pythons were well-rehearsed and insistent. Aurélio, an impatient ball of energy, gave them a few centimes.

'These blacks, they never want to work. It's "Gi' me money, gi' me money" the whole time.'

Aurélio Silva Bordadagua was an old African hand. Short, powerfully built, balding, with well-kept moustache and beard, check shirt, moccasin shoes, he was one of that legion of bullhearted, indefatigable men and women who for five centuries have been emigrating from a life of thankless, backbreaking hard work in Portugal to a life of scarcely less thankless, backbreaking hard work in the tropics, in Goa, Rio de Janeiro, Caracas or Luanda.

A century ago in British Guiana and other dominions of the snobbish and race-conscious English to which they went as indentured labourers they would have been treated with disdain. These men, whose ancestors had explored the world from Labrador to the Cape when England was a struggling offshore kingdom, were obliged to occupy a position a degree or two above the blacks but several degrees below any Northern European white.

Aurélio had been a wireless operator in the army which fought hard in Mozambique to keep the Portuguese flag flying. He had gone back to Lisbon, married, fathered a daughter but was back now on a long contract in the continent that mesmerized him. Nourished by *bacalhau*, the dried cod which he adored and which he brought back every so often from Lisbon in his suitcase, Aurélio seemed to be the only source of any initiative in the sleepy apathetic town, a well of African hopelessness.

His job was to supervise the reconstruction of the fort of São João Baptista de Ajudá, St John the Baptist of Whydah. For centuries after the Portuguese had been chased from the rest of the Slave Coast by stronger colonialist powers the little fort had continued to fly the Portuguese flag. The size of a small market garden, it remained a little patch of Portugal, usually surrounded by territory claimed by France. In 1961 the army of Dahomey, now an independent republic free of direct French control, overpowered the tiny garrison and seized the fort. The Portuguese commander was packed off in a taxi over the Nigerian border to Lagos. Portugal, under its own dictator Salazar, sulked but could do nothing.

A quarter of a century later with the blessing of Benin's dictator Portugal in the person of Aurélio was back, paying for the reconstruction of the mouldering walls, remounting the ancient rusting cannon which lay in piles half-buried in the earth and turning the site into a monument to Portuguese history. The governor's house decorated with blue Portuguese *azulejo* tiles was being refurbished and ancient maps framed and hung on its walls. The Portuguese foreign minister had just come out from

19

Lisbon to visit the works and had been well pleased. Benin, with little of its own to celebrate, is constrained to commemorate its former colonial masters and their trade in Beninese slaves.

Apart from the reconstruction of the fort there was no other enterprise of note being undertaken in this poor and tragic place. The atmosphere in Whydah was one of forlorn resignation.

Olaudah Equiano survived to buy his freedom, prosper by his business acumen and influence the course of history by publishing in 1789 a best-selling book which was one of the most powerful testimonies against slavery. He converted to Anglicanism and in 1792 at Soham in Cambridgeshire married Miss Cullen, daughter of James and Ann Cullen, late of Ely.

'Did I consider myself an European,' he wrote, 'I might say my sufferings were great; but when I compare my lot with that of my countrymen, I regard myself as a *particular favourite of Heaven*.

In as much as they helped create the West Indies, his sufferings as he went in to slavery on the other side of the Atlantic and those of millions like him were not in vain: in any case he knew that he was well out of West Africa. Thiam, my guide in Benin, understood his feeling. His brother, who made a living as a football coach, had long ago emigrated to Munich where he was married to a German woman. Thiam wanted to follow him.

'Praise God!'
  'Praise Jesus!'
  'Praise God!'
  'Praise Jesus!'
  'Praise the Lord!'
The shouted antiphon came strong and rhythmic from behind the walls of the chapel. Hurricane Gilbert had passed this way and taken off the roof so the invocations went straight up to heaven.
  'Praise God!'
  'Praise Jesus!'
  'Praise God!'
  'Praise Jesus!'
  'Praise God!'
  'Praise the Lord!'
  'Praise God!'

'Praise Jesus!'

The occasional variation, like the erratic note in a drum solo, gave a touch of interest and of the unforeseen to the chorus. The single-minded Sunday commitment to the Almighty did not prevent the praisers peeping unselfconsciously and curiously at the white man and the wheezing taxi which had pulled into their remote and untidy tin-roofed village.

This, at last, was Accompong Town in the Land of Look Behind.

Ninety minutes before, I had been on the north coast of Jamaica, a place of exceptional natural beauty with its green cliffs and blue sea. Once it had been an enclave of aristocratic refinement where English planters built their palaces. Plantation houses, such as Rose Hall, had been erected there; Noël Coward had lived and was buried there. Now it had been absorbed into the voracious empire of international tourism. I had fled the resort hotel where 172 Austrian insurance agents and their wives had been raucously enjoying a buffet lunch of very modest culinary quality beside the pool. The agents and their wives, lobster-faced in the sun, guffawed merrily as the Jamaican DJ, perfectly attuned to what the guests wanted, persuaded volunteers to limbo and, to the sound of reggae records, inch their white bellies under the pole.

The exercise was a striking, touching example of transatlantic understanding. Few who saw the sight and were able to imagine Fritzi and Greta poring over their home videos of their Caribbean holiday on cold nights in Vienna could have a doubt about the splendid future of Austro-Jamaican relations.

I wanted to meet the Maroons whose ancestors had been among the first to arrive in the Western hemisphere from the Slave Coast and who had been among the first to cut free from slavery and make their own lives. It was not easy to find. The taxi driver 'sorta knew where i' was'. Once he left the main road from Montego Bay he got hopelessly lost in the lanes of the Cockpit Country, a wilderness of conical hills which from the air look like the surface of the human brain. It was never possible to see more than 100 yards ahead and one's sense of direction soon became totally disoriented. The majority of the Jamaicans we saw on the way were turned out in the extreme civilized respectability of their Sunday best, dark suits for the men and dark dresses with demure white hats for the women. They contrasted strangely with the short shorts and bare navels of the happy Austrian barbarians in the hotel. They gave charming but contradictory directions.

'Hello, whitey,' shouted the kids cheerily as we lurched through the villages.

The taxi ended by by twisting and turning down an overgrown track where the overhanging vegetation seemed to be barring our path. Accompong Town, when we found it, could have been in another country. Here lived a centuries-old community bound together by that strongest of bonds, an inherited historical tradition backed by useful tax incentives.

Accompong Town sits in the hills behind the north coast with magnificent views to the far north-eastern horizon, strangely aloof from the rest of the country.

'I had the feeling that the Maroons lived on a raft sailing high above the dark river bed of Jamaican life. And looking out of the window of the shanty in the early morning at the descending layers of mist that were entangled in the millions of leaves, a whole world seemed to separate us from the plains,'

commented Patrick Leigh Fermor on his visit to the village in *The Traveller's Tree*.

'Maroon life unfolds in an airy floating world of its own that has no particular link with any definite place or century.'

It has not changed much in the four decades since he was there. I had a letter of introduction to the Colonel of the Maroons from a Jamaican friend in the BBC. At seventy Martin Luther Wright was upright and alert, every inch a colonel, proud of the fact that his 1,200 Maroons had twice elected him to the colonelcy. He welcomed me to Accompong Town with a warm cordiality understandably admixed with a shrewd assessment of what benefit a foreign journalist's visit might bring his people.

His people are a people of tradition. If that phrase conjures up some prissy conservative religious sect, it does not fit the Maroons. Theirs is a tradition of independence born of warfare;

22

of warfare and victory against the white man. That the Maroon victories happened two or three centuries ago takes away none of their savour. Their hero is their late leader Captain Kojo, brother of another famous Maroon chieftain, Accompong. He was a man who kept the whites and slavery at bay.

We went into the Colonel's friendly, untidy house. After some rummaging he fished out a framed copy of the treaty of 1739 between the Maroons and the British. It was signed after Kojo had fought the redcoats to a standstill and it has its importance in Accompong Town to this day.

We wandered over to Captain Kojo's Health Clinic, a clean modern building decorated with strong vivid murals. It stocked a supply of medicines but had no resident doctor.

'It would be good if we had a doctor . . .', said the Colonel.

The implication was that anyone with friends at the BBC and the money to fly to Jamaica and hire a taxi as far as Accompong Town had enough influence to get the government to send a doctor to live in the village.

'. . . and a telephone.'

The Maroons were people of account well before the English arrived in Jamaica in Oliver Cromwell's time. Though they had discovered it, the Spaniards did not begin settling Jamaica till 1509. They started bringing in black slaves in 1517 to provide labour which the Arawak, in process of annihilation like many of their Amerindian cousins, were unable to provide. Used not as plantation labour, but as cowboys for herding the animals which were the principal wealth of the island, the blacks in Jamaica were better placed than many in America to gallop off and found their own independent societies free of their European masters.

Admiral Penn and General Venables arrived off Jamaica with their 8,000 men and thirty-eight ships in 1655 having failed to take Santo Domingo from the Spaniards. If they were not to return empty-handed after commanding the biggest overseas expedition ever mounted till then by England, they had to conquer something for the Commonwealth. In this ill-regarded and semi-abandoned colony of Spain there were already communities of runaway slaves, the *cimarrones*, living in the wild.

One of their number, Juan de Bolas, helped the English invaders to clear the last Spaniards from the island and in 1663 was granted the rank of Colonel. The bulk of the Maroons, however, despised the idea of living under English rule as much as they had despised the thought of living under Spain, and wanted nothing better than to live a life of freedom out of the range of any European government. They rejected the offer of the rights and privileges of the subjects of His Majesty and twenty acres of land each which was made to them by Sir Charles Lyttleton, the Lieutenant-Governor, and they destroyed the settlements of any colonist who sought to live too close to their own hunting grounds. They eventually ambushed and killed de Bolas too.

The island began to grow richer under the English with the sort of sugar-cane plantations which were to make the West Indies incomparably wealthy and important to the colonial powers over the next century, and the independence of the Maroons and the bad example it gave to slaves on the plantations began to irk the English. By the 1730s the colony was practically in a state of guerrilla warfare as the planters battled to impose themselves on the blacks who overwhelmingly outnumbered them. It was a war, moreover, where the sweating and malaria-ridden English regiments were at a disadvantage faced with black communities of runaways who knew every inch of their own territory.

The runaways who had survived the voyage from the Slave Coast, Ibos, Mandingos, Ashantis, or native Jamaicans guessed that there would be no help for them till they came together under one leader to face the white man. This they did in 1730. Kojo was a squat, powerful man whose musculature made some who saw him believe he was a hunchback. A contemporary sketch shows him dressed in a shirt and in a pair of trousers which came down to the top of his very powerful calves. He is barefoot carrying a musket, pouches for powder and shot, and a small cutlass.

Like every guerrilla force which has ever taken the field against a stronger enemy, Kojo's Maroons had to pit intelligence against superior firepower.

Weapons were a problem. With no means of making their own guns or powder they seized muskets from the soldiers who fell to them or who dumped their arms as they ran. Prizing what they had, they worked at their marksmanship trying harder than their adversaries to make every shot find its mark. Their fieldcraft was superb. Well after the first Maroon war was over a Maroon band gave a demonstration of their skills to the Governor. The eighteenth-century historian Edward Long wrote:

'With amazing ability they ran, or rather rolled, through their various firings and evolutions. This part of their exercise indeed more justly deserves to be stiled evolution than any that is practised by regular troops, for they fire stooping almost to the very ground, and no sooner are their muskets discharged than they throw themselves into a thousand antic gestures, and tumble over and over, so as to elude the shot as well as to deceive the aim of their adversaries which their nimble and almost instantaneous change of position renders extremely uncertain.'

They were masters of the ambush. Covered with greenery they would stand stock-still within a yard of a redcoat till the moment of attack had arrived.

They sounded the alarm with the *abeng*, a cow horn whose sound would carry across the hills of the Cockpit Country, warning of the approach of the English or summoning reinforcements or even calling a specific individual in code.

The English had to bring in Indians and their tracker dogs from the Mosquito Coast of Central America but, though they did better than the redcoats, even they were incapable of reducing Kojo and his forces.

The exhausted English decided to call a truce. On 1 March 1739 under a large cotton tree at Petty River Bottom, Colonel Guthrie and Captain Sadler concluded a pact with Kojo which gave the Maroons freedom (which they already had), 1,500 acres of land in perpetuity, permission to hunt more or less where they wanted and the guarantee of justice for any injury done against them by a European. In exchange – and here came the rub – they were to hunt down rebels and runaway slaves. That bargain has not yet been forgotten by the black majority in Jamaica, a fact which probably explains why none of the Maroon leaders has yet been honoured in independent Jamaica.

Thomas Thistlewood, a young Englishman who came to Jamaica to seek his fortune, has left a casual but at times horrifying record of the fate that the slaves were condemned to but which the Maroons were spared. Thistlewood was to meet the Maroon leader, now more than seventy years old, a decade after his armistice. According to his diary, on Thursday, 29 May 1750 on the road to St James,

> 'Between 8 and 9 miles from Dean's Valley, met Colonel Cudjoe, one of his wives, one of his sons, a Lieutenant and other attendants. He shook me by the hand, and begged a dram of us, which we gave him. He had on a feather hat, sword by his side, gun upon his shoulder, &c. Barefoot and barelegged, somewhat a majestic look. He bought to my memory the picture of Robinson Crusoe.'

The next year Thistlewood was installed as the employee of a large plantation owner. Making an official return of slaves and cattle for tax purposes, he met Accompong, Kojo's brother at the town of Lacovia.

> 'Capt. Compoon here, about my size, in a ruffled shirt, blue broad cloth coat, scarlet cuff to his sleeves, gold buttons, & he had with white cap, and black hat, white linen breeches puffed at the rims, no stockings or shoes on. Many of his wives, and his son there.'

The Maroons were right to value their freedom. Thistlewood's diaries for a typical week at the end of July 1756 coolly recorded the punishments and degradations that faced a recaptured slave. Port Royal, a runaway, had been recaptured.

> 'Gave him a moderate whipping, pickled him well, made Hector shit in his mouth, immediately put in a gag whilst his mouth was full & made him wear it 4 or 5 hours.'

A few days later two other runaways were caught.

> 'Friday, 30th July 1756: Punch catched at Salt River and brought home. Flogged him and Quacoo well, and then washed and rubbed in salt pickle, lime juice & bird pepper; also whipped Hector for losing his hoe, made New Negro Joe piss in his eyes & mouth &c.'

Two days later Hazat, a slave who had been at liberty since

April, was seized.

> 'Put him in the bilboes both feet; gagged him; locked his hands together; rubbed him with molasses & exposed him naked to the flies all day, and to the mosquitoes all night, without fire'.

Thistlewood had the run of every female slave he fancied and he recorded his activity in scraps of Latin. At the end of 1753 when he was thirty-three he started a relationship with Phibbah which was to continue for many years. She was one among many.

The next year his diary reads, for instance,

> 'Tuesday, 19th February 1754: At night *Cum* Phibbah, *Sup. me. lect*.

> Thursday, 21st February: p.m. *Cum* Phibbah. *Illa habet menses*.

> Friday, 22nd February: At night *Cum* Phibbah.

> Sunday, 24th February: At night *Cum* Phibbah.

> Monday 25th February: At night *Cum* Phibbah.

> Tuesday 26th February: Phibbah keep away.

> Thursday, 28th February: *Cum* Phibbah.

> Friday, 1st March: p.m. *Cum* Phibbah . . . and, in the evening, *Cum* Susanah in the curing-house, *stans*.'

Five years later there was still much to confide to the diary. On 21 June 1759 there was a christening at a neighbouring plantation and Phibbah went there to help cook the dinner but Thistlewood had much to do on his own plantation. In the early afternoon a runaway slave was brought back by boat.

> 'Abba in the canoe, flogged her well.
> About 2 p.m. *Cum* Mazerine, *Sup. Terr*. old curing-house

canepiece. Gave her a *bitt* [coin].
About 3 p.m. *Cum* Warsoe, in the boiling house.
Stans: Backwards.'

In August Thistlewood in the midst of much entertaining of his planter neighbours records,

'Sunday, 12th: a.m. *Cum* Little Lydde, *Sup. Terr.* Gave her a *bitt* . . .

Friday 17th: At night *Cum* Mountain Susanah, *Sup. me. lect.* gave her 2 *bitts* . . .

Wednesday 22nd: a.m. *Cum* Violet *Sup. Terr.* Gave her a *bitt* . . .

Wednesday 29th: *Cum* Mould's Lydde, in the curing-house, Stans! Backwd.

Tuesday, 4th September: In the evening *Cum* Egypt Susanah, *Sup. me. lect.* Gave her 2 *bitts*. Sent word by her to Phib., she might come if she would, and accordingly she did. At night *Cum* Phib.'

Half a century after Kojo signed his peace there was another Maroon War. This time the men of Accompong Town were no longer interested in fighting the colonial masters, indeed some, standing by the 1739 treaty, took the English side against the Maroons of neighbouring Trelawny Town. They were even awarded some of their neighbours' land. The survivors of the defeated Maroons were shipped off to exile, first in icy Nova Scotia, and later in Sierra Leone.

Kojo's memory is alive in Accompong Town. Every 6 January the hero's birthday is celebrated. The senior Maroons gather in Kojo's cave for a conclave and when they emerge the locals and the visitors get down to a vast feast. There is the roasted flesh of male animals and enough rum to last into the night and on to the next day.

'You must come back and see us on 6 January,' said the Colonel. 'Then we'll have some fun.'

Chapter Two

Cuba

'Once the United States is in Cuba, who will get it out?'

José Martí.

... VII. That to enable the United States to maintain the independence of Cuba, and to protect the people thereof, as well as for its defense, the government of the Cuba will sell or lease to the United States lands necessary for coaling or naval stations at certain specified points, to be agreed upon with the President of the United States.'

The Platt Amendment, adopted as an annex to
the Constitution of Cuba, 1901.

Bearing an introduction to a Ghanaian, I had arrived on the Isle of Youth after an efficient and punctual half-hour flight from Havana. We had flown aboard a small Russian Antonov airliner across the wasp waist of Cuba over neat circular fields each irrigated by a gantry which rotated like the hand of some enormous clock. During the thirty minutes a smiling hostess had managed to fit three separate services – boiled sweets, a soft drink and strong sweet coffee.

'There are thirty-three different nations represented on our island,' said the black woman taxi driver proudly as we bowled along in the heat of the afternoon from the little airport towards the town of Nueva Gerona. Only the obstinately purblind visitor could be oblivious of the high calling which Comandante en Jefe Fidel Castro Ruz had bestowed on this once ill-regarded island.

A dozen enormous hoardings along the road told in graphic form the history of the island, from discovery by Columbus to the change of name from the Isle of Pines and its establishment as a centre for the education of an international elite of anti-imperialist youth.

This is where Fidel Castro has set out his grand design, the gesture with which he and Cuba plan, with the power of reason and literacy and the education of tens of thousands of young people drawn from the poorest countries, to change the world.

The idea of the island becoming an educational powerhouse for the Third World surfaced in 1977 when Castro offered Agostinho Neto, the president of the newly independent Angola, places for 600 Angolan children. At any one time the island contained nearly 20,000 foreign students, young Namibian boys and girls of less than ten getting the sort of schooling that would be impossible to obtain in their South African occupied homeland, Grenadians training in disciplines that have been banned in their island since the US invasion of 1983, Mozambicans and Angolans working at their books away from the threat of war and famine, a sprinkling of young people from Francophone Africa, a big contingent of Ghanaians, some Ethiopians, a few Nigerians, some Seychellois . . .

After a period of instruction in Spanish the students graduate to the score of *Institutos Politécnicos* where they live in spartan conditions, are fed and receive a small monthly amount of pocket money. They are expected, too, to devote a few hours a day to working in the fields on the project of making the island into one vast fruit farm.

The Isle of Youth is a strange place. It lies where the sea and the land dissolve into one another in shoals, reefs and shallows to fool the senses and bewitch the imagination. As you stand by the seashore it is at times impossible to distinguish what is above the greeny-blue opaline water and what below.

This subtle mixture of sea and land fooled Columbus himself when he cruised across it in 1494 on his second voyage. As he passed a chain of cays which he called the Gardens of the Queen he was convinced that land stretched uninterruptedly to the west and that therefore he was off the coast of Asia and not far from his goal, the court of the Great Khan. Accordingly on 12 June he ordered his *escribano* Juan Pérez de Luna to draw up a solemn document attesting to the fact that the southern coast of Cuba was part of the mainland of Asia and prescribing punishment for anyone who alleged it was not. The day after he ordered the document drawn up he discovered an island, generally low lying but sprinkled with the occasional strange mountainous outcrops. He went to his grave, they say, convinced against all subsequent evidence, that in these waters he had completed the great enterprise of changing world history and had established the passage to the Indies as Ferdinand and Isabella had commissioned him to do.

In choosing the Isle of Pines for his attempt to change world history Castro was, perhaps unconsciously, following Columbus' example. Perhaps the Cuban was determined on the political purification of an island which had fallen into a state of imperialist mortal sin and had to redeem itself from its wicked past. It had after all served as a place of exile for the young José Martí, the apostle of Cuban independence from Spain, who in 1870 during Spanish colonial times was sentenced to six years in prison at the age of seventeen for his anti-Spanish activities. After the US forces had intervened in Cuba in 1898 and finally crushed the Spanish colonial rule which had already been mortally weakened by the Cuban insurgents, Washington set its heart on acquiring the Isle of Pines. For two decades US diplomats tried to prise it away from the new Cuban republic, and a US land company attempted to foment a rebellion in the island against Havana in 1905 which was intended to give the excuse for a US military intervention. Cuba was confirmed in possession of it only in 1926, the year of Castro's birth.

It was a handy place to keep criminals and in 1931 the dictator Geratdo Machado built the *presidio* or prison there, and the circular panopticons with room for 5,000 inmates remain now as a museum a kilometre or two outside Nueva Gerona. Later under the tyrant Batista its listless economy was given a boost when the island became a duty-free port. Castro himself was sent to the *presidio* with twenty-three companions after his conviction for the assault on Batista's troops in the Moncada barracks in Santiago in 1953. The *presidio*, it was said, was the real birthplace of the rebel army which was finally to vanquish Batista in January 1959. There, though Castro himself was held in solitary confinement for some months, the insurgent companions could organize and plan together for the future. He still loves to show his guests around and tell them what a good plate of spaghetti he used to cook there.

One suspects that Castro's choice of the island is also intended to avenge the personal discomfort that he himself suffered on its soil. The concept is a heroic and generous one. But, as I was to see, the high purposes of the Cuban leader, on this island as on Cuba itself, are sometimes brought low by the reality of base human nature. It took a little time however for me to realize that the apple of discord was also ripening amid the citrus groves.

Nueva Gerona itself was something of a disappointment after those high-sounding hoardings. A dusty place of modest, mainly single-storey buildings, some with shady colonnades, and one or two nondescript squares, built near a creek jammed with shabby fishing vessels. Nothing of the glory of colonial architecture to be found in Havana, little obvious sign of the sublime calling of revolutionary pedagogy, just the odd cafeteria and the usual run of Cuban shops containing few if any attractive goods. One of the few spruce-looking places was the *diplotienda*, the dollar shop, cool, air-conditioned and discreetly sited in a side street.

'There are young people from thirty-three different countries studying here,' said the local television producer with the same genuine pride that the taxi driver had expressed. But Gerona's pride is mingled with impatience verging on hostility to the *prietos*, the blacks.

'There are a lot of *prietos* here. This isn't quite the place for people like us, particularly for a person like me.' Laura, white-skinned and with peroxided hair with black roots, worked in the Savings Bank. She wore her skin colouring like other women would wear some exquisite gem, something to be valued enormously in a country where, sadly, there were so many of those rough *prietos*. She talked in a tone which took for granted that I, a fellow white, would understand. The *prietos* were, after all, doubly embarrassing, reminding Cuba of its barbaric slave past and at the same time threatening the whites with a fatal, ineradicable admixture of black blood after some casual copulation.

'We used to live in Havana, you know, but we got offered this big house and we came. Housing is such a problem in Havana but I think we'll go back before long. Havana is so much nicer.' There was more than a touch of Lady Bracknell about Laura. Her husband Rodolfo, moustachioed, sallower, South European looking but still a man with no obvious negroid features, worked in the post office. He was an eager, vigorous, friendly man of perhaps rather limited intelligence.

We sat over supper – fried steak and fried plantain, boiled rice and sauce, washed down with delicious cold home-made lemonade from the Russian fridge – in the kitchen of their small three-bedroomed house with a yard where a pig lurked. Four-year-old Richard played and shouted at our feet. The *prietos*, especially foreign *prietos* straight from Africa, were clearly a problem for Laura and Rodolfo.

'All that money they have', she said. 'It's not right.'

They were a problem, too, even for Ernesto the television journalist at Isla Visión. 'You have to teach them everything. Many of them when they came used to eat with their hands, you know. There are only a few cafes here. They come here and, well, you know . . .' His voice tailed off. Like Laura he took it for granted that I would understand and sympathize. Fidel's grand international designs were, as on so many previous occasions, being caught in the tough brambles of incorrigible human nature.

Nor did the brambles grow on only one side of the fence.

'I did not come to Cuba in order to work in the fields', said the Malian. 'I do not work in the fields, whatever they say. They call me a black dog but I *will not* work in the fields.'

The man from Mali, a man from Benin and I were standing at the entrance to one of the *Institutos Politécnicos* as the evening sun set over the island. The *IP* was a modern three-storey building on an H-shaped plan built on a gentle rise overlooking the rolling plains outside Nueva Gerona. A mile or so to the east on another rise stood another *Instituto Politécnico* and on the horizon another. The Cuban flag hung from a high flagpole in the yard in which some Nicaraguans were playing football.

'Look,' the Malian said in the same Lady Bracknell tone of uttermost disgust as I had heard from Laura, 'there are fields all around us.'

So there were. Uncleared fields full of weeds or thorny bush and tidier fields planted with citrus trees. On the horizon was the

33

factory where the best quality fruit was packed and the remainder transformed into every sort of by-product that could be expected from a grapefruit or an orange.

I had met Jean-Claude, the Béninois, the man from the Slave Coast, earlier in the day in the main street of Gerona as I sought out the Ghanaians. Dressed in brightly patterned West African dress and in his early twenties, he was, I thought, surely a Ghanaian student.

'I am from Benin,' he said gravely. 'I will take you to the Ghanaians. But you must come to my school first.'

Once I launched into French the conversation took off. Our shared mastery of the French subjunctive bound us as tightly together as Laura had assumed she and I were linked in our common whiteness. After a period learning Spanish in Havana, Jean-Claude was now in the second year of a veterinary science course. He did not like Cuba.

'In my country the sons of politicians get sent to the United States or Moscow. The rest of us come to places like this.' His distaste was that of a Parisian chef presented with a doner kebab in some greasy North London cafe.

In the taxi Jean-Claude produced a litany of complaints against his present conditions of life. There was no money; the teachers were too young; they often made mistakes; the food was lousy; there was racism. There was little – nothing – to recommend it. Fidel's high purpose was being shipwrecked on the protests of one of its supposed beneficiaries.

Twenty minutes out of the town we got to the *Instituto Politécnico*. A mound of kitchen garbage lay where the taxi driver grumpily dumped us.

'My problem is that I've done so long here that I can't afford to go home. I've got to stay and complete my studies.'

We climbed up the grimy staircase with no balustrade to the big, bare dormitory where Jean-Claude lived, studied and slept with several hundred others. His territory was a large wooden wardrobe and the lower of two bunks. Presumably because it was a Saturday few others were about.

'People don't live like this in my country,' he said.

I did not believe him.

'Can you give me a few dollars? You can't buy anything here without dollars.'

34

To judge by the slogans on the walls the morale of some of the Southern Africans was much higher. Mottos and slogans praising SWAPO and Che Guevara were much in evidence on the walls towards what was evidently the more Namibian end of the dormitory.

'Perhaps it's better for the Southern Africans. If they didn't come here they wouldn't have anything. Their countries are at war.

'But for us, there is nothing to do here. *Absolument rien à faire*. Sometimes we get a football team together with the Anglophones – the Nigerians and Ghanaians. But there's nothing really to do.' Here Jean-Claude, the Francophone, adopted son of 1,000 years of French culture, reasserted his values over those of his poor brother Africans condemned to drag out their lives speaking mere English or Portuguese. But there was another French speaker with him.

'Look at him, he's the only Malian.'

From a lower bunk a pair of legs emerged. Then the trunk and head of the sad, lonely but defiant African. As the three of us left the *Politécnico*, the Malian delivered his Philippic against work in the fields. I thought about the gulf between Castro's ideals and imperfect men and women on whom he has to rely to carry them out. The Cuban leader in grand gesture is opening his country, devoting his teachers and welcoming poor students from all over the Third World in the noble cause of promoting social justice. And all that many of those involved could do was complain.

Was the Cuban leader no less misinformed about human nature on the Isle of Youth than Columbus had been about its geography? Was the New Man that Cuban socialism was to mould and perfect any less of a delusion than the idea that Cuba formed part of the continent of Asia?

Havana was different. More than any other city of America Havana is Spain beyond the sea. Of the Spanish Americans the Colombians may claim to speak a purer Castilian than the rest, Cartagena may claim to be the perfect Spanish colonial city. There may be more descendants of Spaniards in Argentina. Santo Domingo may have Spanish buildings of greater age. But Havana, for better or worse, is more Spanish. Spain, routed by local militias in South America and Mexico, was kicked out of most of its empire in the first decade or two of the nineteenth century. But to Cuba, and its capital, Spain clung with the passion and ferocity of a nation in decline, with the intense but forlorn love of an ageing woman for an only remaining son or for a wayward but irreplaceable lover. It is nearly a century since the Spaniards were finally forced out of Cuba but the Spanish past is still there.

The old Spanish nature of the city does not, it must be said, reveal itself to the newly arrived visitor immediately. Those coming by air from abroad are received at José Martí airport in a brand new international terminal brightly lit, air-conditioned, painted in soft colours and bespeaking the quiet efficiency that all airlines aspire to.

There are handcarts for luggage. The immigration is thorough but rapid with the booth in which you present your passport provided with a mirror installed behind your head in which the immigration office can survey your back and any luggage you bring. The route through customs is quick and nonchalant. The National Bank has a booth where you can change your foreign currency into the overvalued Cuban *pesos* which bear the portraits of revolutionary heroes and scenes of gallantry from Castro's war against the tyrant Batista.

Outside, the terminal pretence ends. There takes over a particularly Cuban blend of Third World lack of development and state control of what development there is. This insures that the basics of life are provided for all citizens but that insufficient stimulus is given to workers to ensure that duties are carried out in an efficient manner.

Such an observation is offered in no supercilious or carping spirit for the way of life it implies has much to recommend it.

In Havana unlike at other airports in Latin America, there is no need for child beggars or destitute invalids to beg for your coin outside the doors of the terminal; no taxi drivers, desperate for a fare, need fight among themselves over your body; nor are you conscious of having to guard your possessions at every second lest they be made away with by some wretch to whom they represent the day's only chance of getting a square meal. And the police presence is powerful enough, in this spot at least, for no touts dare to offer you publicly the black market rate of five or six times more *pesos* for your dollars than the National Bank had offered you a moment before.

Instead you are offered, if there is one available at the moment, the choice of a Turistaxi for which you will have to pay in dollars or a Cubatur coach which will take you to your hotel in its chauffeur's own good time and not before. Sit back and you will lose nothing, fret and fume and you are condemned to frustration.

Perhaps the Spanishness of Cuba first betrays itself on the drive into Havana. The main road leads to the city through gentle, seductive, warm, lush, verdant landscape of a sort nowhere to be found in Spain with tropical vegetation, sugar cane and tall graceful palm trees. But there is something Spanish in the propaganda messages which, as in Nueva Gerona, declaim every few hundred yards to the new arrival their admiration of bravery, the cult of the hero, the love of the rhetorical.

Their tone of nationalism, devotion to Fidel and defiance of the Yankee, though not their clever modern typography, is reminiscent of bullfight posters. Fidel and Che, and occasionally Camilo Cienfuegos, are billed the *toreros* who are risking or who have risked their lives against the dangerous beast of imperialism. Castro was, after all, the son of a Spanish soldier who settled on the island. Che was an adventurous doctor from Buenos Aires who quit his native Argentina to throw in his lot with the revolutionary Castro. Camilo was the laughing young worker who was wounded in the war against Batista and who disappeared in mysterious circumstances shortly after Castro took power in 1959.

Across the Plaza de la Revolución, the arena for Castro's flights of oratory, down the hill between the Napoleonic Museum and the Grecian façade of the University, the city stretches out to the Caribbean Sea. Havana has certainly come down in the world. It was made to suffer by Castro from the first days of the Revolution. It was denied paint and wood and bricks and nails so that the underprivileged countryside could benefit, and perhaps also so that it should atone for the shameful days of Batista when it was the brothel and gambling joint *par excellence* of the Caribbean.

But, dowdy and unkempt, the city still continues to draw in people from the rest of the country, including the now overprivi-

leged countryside, like a magnet. Dirty, unpainted and ill cared
for as much of it is, the Cuban capital could well pass for some
seedy Spanish Mediterranean port of the late 1940s when Franco
was in power and things were hard as Spain was being boycotted
by the victorious allies.

Old Havana, Habana la Vieja, the nucleus of the old Spanish
capital, bursts with humanity. Every last room in every last
house seems to be filled with people. The once proud patios of
beautiful palaces of Spanish notables are grimy now. One particularly handsome palace is an office for the traffic police, others
are turned into tenements, rats' nests worn with the daily passage of the humble Cubans packed into them. Living in a tightly
packed promiscuity which used to be the price of inhabiting any
walled city, the inhabitants, some black, some white, peer out at
you from behind unpainted grills, they look down on you from
wobbly balconies, they watch you from doorways as you pass,
you look into their bedrooms from the pavement.

The only palace which still serves an original function is the
archbishop's residence, a light, airy old building on the corner of
Chacón constructed round a patio full of plants and flowers.
From there the young and handsome Archbishop Jaime Ortega
manages the tricky relationship between Church and State as his
predecessors have done for centuries.

Every so often traffic in the narrow cobbled streets is cut off
by mounds of sand and bags of cement where the *microbrigadas*
are at work, the voluntary unpaid and unskilled groups of
workers sent out from each office and factory to try and build
dwellings for distribution among the staff of their establishment.

Everywhere in the old city is the stamp of Spain. The street
names, each carried on a wrought-iron plaque, have been un-
changed for centuries: Amargura – Bitterness Street; Obispo –
Bishop Street; Mercaderes – Merchants' Street; Sol – Sun
Street; Luz – Light Street. Many of the street corners retain the
decorated slabs of cast iron set there to protect the bricks on the
corner from damage by passing wagon wheels. By the railway
station there is a small stretch of the city wall still to be seen.

Havana is still recognizably the colonial fortress where every
year the treasure ships assembled to convoy the wealth of the
Indies back to fill Spain's exhausted coffers. The port is still the
magnificently wide, deep and well protected harbour, separated

from the sea by a narrow and easily defended channel, where the galleons assembled from Vera Cruz in Mexico, from Portobello and Cartagena in the southern Caribbean. From Havana they would sail eastwards together defying the French, Dutch and British fleets which lay in wait for them and occasionally captured them.

The entrance to the channel which leads into the harbour is to this day controlled by the twin forts of The Three Kings, commonly known as El Morro, on the tip of the hill which rises on the east bank and La Punta on the flat west bank beside the city itself. Some historians describe them as monuments to Sir Francis Drake. In the late sixteenth century the city, small but already rich and important, was seized with fear at the thought of being attacked by Drake, who had already 'singed the King of Spain's beard' in 1587 by destroying ships in the harbour of Cadiz. From everywhere on the island and from as far away as Mexico people came to defend Havana and its few hundred Spanish families. The authorities even declared an amnesty for fugitives from the law so that they would return and swell the garrison. El Morro and La Punta took shape but Drake sailed by without attacking the city.

In the centre of the old city is the castle of La Fuerza. However terrible the events that took place inside it, it is a jewel of a building. Its smooth, white stone walls rise out of the waters of a quiet moat, their angles calculated for lines of defensive fire with all the skill a modern engineer would put into a skyscraper. Built on the plan of a four-leaved clover it was started in 1562 but took twenty years to finish. In 1574 the architect Francisco Calona complained that no one on the job had been paid for thirty months and that at least 30,000 ducats were owing.

When La Fuerza was completed Philip II was very proud of it and commanded the best mason in Seville to carve his coat of arms on a stone which would be put over the main gate. The stone is still there. The shield is engraved with the castles of Castille, the lions of León, the chains of the Basque Country, the bars of Aragon and Catalonia, the pomegranate of Granada, the *fleur de lys* of France, all surrounded by the collar of the Order of the Golden Fleece, its sheepskin hanging limp at the bottom, one of the oldest and best pieces of sculpture in the island.

Fifty years after it was completed a delicate cylindrical bell tower was added to the western bastion of La Fuerza and on it was perched a graceful little weathervane. The bronze figure of a woman, *La Giraldilla*, hand on hip carrying the insignia of the Order of Calatrava, has for centuries been the symbol and mascot of Havana.

The British returned with greater success in 1762. Britain and Spain were engaged in a war in which Spain was hoping to recover Gibraltar. Britain for its part sent Admiral Sir George Pocock across the Atlantic to capture once and for all the Key of the Indies. Two hundred ships were manned by 8,226 sailors and carried 12,041 soldiers, the largest armed force ever to go to war in the New World. After much delay English troops started attacking the landward site of El Morro. It fell, despite the bravery of its commander, a naval officer, Captain Luis de Velasco, who fell mortally wounded in its defence. You can still see the point at which the redcoats pierced the walls. Havana itself surrendered on 14 August, two months after the British had landed. The effect on the prestige of Spain must have been similar to that suffered by the British when Singapore fell in World War II. Not only had Charles III of Spain not recovered Gibraltar, he had lost the strongest fortress in America.

The booty was tremendous as the goods in the city were put on public auction. It raised £750,000. Albemarle and Pocock each received £150,000 while every sailor and every soldier was given £4.4.9¾d and £4.1.8½d respectively. The two countries signed a peace treaty and a much poorer city was returned to Spain inside a year. All Spain got out of the episode was a new hero. It was decreed that thereafter one Spanish warship should always bear the name Velasco and one still does.

To prevent El Morro ever being taken unawares again the Spaniards built a new fortress, La Cabaña, on the ridge behind it and its high stone walls now dominate the port and the city. Within them too many men and women have gone to their deaths for political reasons, in colonial times, in the first republic and since Castro came to power.

The religious and civilian architecture of the old city matches the military architecture. Round the corner from La Fuerza is the cathedral.

After three decades of deliberate neglect the government is taking an interest in restoring the historic buildings of Spanish

Havana. In the first days of the Revolution public architecture was bent to glorify the deeds of the revolutionaries. The motor launch *Granma* in which in 1956 Castro and his companions, storm tossed and puking, sailed from Mexico to the Oriente to start a foolhardy invasion of Batista's Cuba, was embalmed and displayed in a pavilion of glass in the Museum of the Revolution. Outside the Museum stands one of the Russian tanks driven by Castro himself in the effort to repel the US invasion of the Bay of Pigs in 1961.

In more recent years what might be called the Leningrad factor has taken over. In Russia the Moscow government decided that no political harm would be done and a healthy nationalism boosted if the glories of Peter the Great's capital, including his very statue, were restored. So, too, with the Cuban Revolution; finally confident that it has established itself sufficiently forcefully for all prospect to have disappeared of any return to the past, the government feels confident enough to face pre-Castro history – or at least the remoter parts of it. Now, with the help of the United Nations, work has started on rescuing the old city.

The splendours of the old city were, like the rest of the Cuban economy, based on the toil of blacks from the Slave Coast and elsewhere in Africa; indeed Havana grew to greatness on slavery. In 1580 Philip II annexed Portugal and thereby took control of the Portuguese slave trade and in 1595 gave one Gómez Reynel permission to import into the Caribbean 4,500 slaves a year for nine years.

That was the making of the city. The new supply of labour allowed the slave masters to make the best of the excellent natural conditions for growing sugar. The Portuguese slave ships brought in a good deal of contraband that Cuba could not obtain from elsewhere and the city made money selling the seamen food and lodging.

Havana, not for the last time in its history, became Sin City. The sailors wanted rum, women and song and the soldiers from the growing military garrison, as badly paid as the builders had been, were a pest. One governor complained to Philip,

'The soldiers live in the greatest licence taking women and slaves from the citizens by force . . . no justice nor magistrate dares go to the meat market or the fish market because

41

no sooner do they arrive than the soldiers break down the doors and take things without weighing or paying; and if anyone says anything to them they threaten to crack the heads of justices and magistrates and that is what they are allowed to do.'

The freedom to import slaves was a constant cry of the Cuban whites. They finally got it in 1791 because the opportunities of making fortunes from sugar were not to be ignored. The blacks in Saint-Domingue across the water to the east had risen up against their French masters and Haïti, the first black republic in the modern world, was on its way to being established. The world's greatest source of sugar was in crisis. An *arroba* of sugar which in 1785 had fetched no more than four *reales* was a few years later selling for up to thirty *reales*. Cuba's future could be brilliant if the labour could be brought in.

In 1791 limitations on the importation of slaves were relaxed, the sugar industry prospered as never before and the proportion of blacks in society grew. As the independence of Haïti was established there was a panic flight of perhaps 30,000 whites from Saint-Domingue to Cuba where the government was happy to receive them. From the Cubans' point of view the new whites would help establish a better racial mix while the fleeing French, traumatized by the slaughter in their own country, and settling in a neighbouring country still controlled by whites, resolved they would never yield to blacks again.

All these facts help to explain why the Cuban middle class stayed loyal to Spain at the beginning of the nineteenth century when the middle classes of the rest of the Spanish empire were seeking independence.

Cuba may not dominate the Caribbean as it once did, but Havana itself, the site the Spaniards chose as their principal base in the Caribbean, is no less important in the scheme of things than it ever was. For three decades it has been the conduit through which the Soviets have supplied Cuba and defied the United States to the point where the world was at one moment on the brink of nuclear war.

Every day oil tankers and cargo vessels from the Soviet Union and Eastern Europe make their way up the channel into the port, keeping the island supplied and alive. Some tie up under La

Cabaña in the shadow of the large statue of Christ which Castro's government has left blessing the scene. The water round the quays are covered with a thick film of oil from the years of spillages as the Soviet tankers unloaded their countless cargoes into the refinery complex on the south side of the harbour. The warehouses bulge with the goods the Soviet Union sends over to keep Cuban industry going. Whereas 300 years ago the harbour saw Spanish convoys gathering to take treasure back to Europe, today the flow is reversed as the Soviets spend their millions of roubles maintaining the Cuban government. Whichever way the goods flow they have to pass under the walls of La Cabaña, beside La Fuerza and between La Punta and El Morro.

At the beginning of the Revolution one warehouse bulged with a particular sort of goods. It was used by the government as a vast second-hand emporium where the personal possessions of those who quit Cuba were put on sale. The emigrants, called *gusanos* or worms by the government, were obliged to relinquish virtually everything of value to the state as they left. With Cuba's foreign exchange reserves falling, the collected items were put on sale to anyone who could pay in dollars. When the scheme first started there were things of great value and big bargains to be had by those who were attracted by the trade and got in quickly. By the time of my first visit in 1963 the remains were a sad jumble of tawdry bric-a-brac, fading women's dresses, useless household implements and rubbish – which must nevertheless have been dear to many families. It did the government no credit and was a lugubrious reminder of the auction by the British two centuries previously.

Castro is vengeful with those who do not support the revolution. One of my sharpest memories of Havana after the mass exodus of thousands of disaffected Cubans through the port of Mariel that Castro permitted in 1980, was of seeing the daubing of the house of one of those who had opted to flee to the United States. '*AQUÍ VIVIÓ UN TRAIDOR HOMOSEXUAL*' they painted in letters a yard high on the wall. '*HERE LIVED A HOMOSEXUAL TRAITOR.*' The house stood at the end of a long straight main road in a busy suburb and was visible to everyone for hundreds of yards; the message could not have been lost on those who remained.

In 1969, well before the Mariel exodus, the Cuban government came to regard the author in a similar light – politically, I add, though not sexually. The *Financial Times*, for whom I was writing at the time, had sent an advertising salesman, a sharp and successful Trinidadian, to Havana. Let him be called Gomes for that was not his name. The energetic and persuasive Gomes convinced the government – as he had already convinced many other governments in the Caribbean and was yet to persuade many more – that their interests would be well served by spending money on buying advertising space in a survey of their country in the newspaper. The investment of the cost of one page of advertising would, Gomes explained allow the *Financial Times* to publish another page of editorial material devoted to them. Gomes, and his colleagues who did similar jobs in other parts of the world, used to make clear that the government they were talking to would have no editorial control over the independent comments of the newspaper – a fact that, they rightly pointed out, would enhance the value of whatever was said. There was, however, a more or less tacit agreement that nothing too damning would be uttered in surveys which were, after all, financed by the country in question. No one pays good money to be vilified.

In 1969 Gomes came to such an arrangement with the Ministry of Foreign Trade in Havana who had an understandable interest in having some pages of an internationally known newspaper devote some considerable space to Cuba at at time when the island was the object of very considerable hostility from the government of the United States.

The enterprise was not to prosper. I was sent to Havana in 1969 to write a survey which would be neither fawning nor censorious but which would be seen by reasonable people as fair. It was the year in which Castro decided that Cuba was to commemorate the century of the first Cuban armed uprising against Spanish imperialism, break all production records and make 10,000,000 tons of sugar in one year. This was literally a superhuman task in a country which had never produced more than 6,000,000 tons of sugar in any year, which was cut off from the United States, the supplier of much of its machinery, and which had to maintain a large defensive army against the risk of a new invasion.

To seek after fairness in such a situation was about as realistic as to ask an Olympic weightlifter about his taste in ties as he prepared for a record lift. The Cuban government wanted encouragement not fairness. At one point they took me to a health centre in the new town of Alamar a few miles to the east of Havana so that I might have the opportunity of admiring the Cuban health service. They were not to know, and I was too reticent to tell them, that few subjects bore me more comprehensively than health. I wrestled to find suitable questions but my plodding enquiries about what illnesses were most troublesome, which had been logged by the official who had been appointed to accompany me, were, I was to learn, taken as insulting or worse. Late one evening I received summons to the Ministry of Foreign Trade and sensed trouble.

I was conducted formally into a bare salon furnished with a chandelier and a few mock Louis XV chairs and into the presence of Marcelo Fernández Font, Minister of Foreign Trade. He was an intense, scholarly looking man with glasses and was, according to his ministerial colleagues, something of a cold fish.

'You have been guilty of provocation. You will leave on the next plane. Until the plane leaves you are free to go where you like,' he said.

Though I had sensed trouble I was at the same time dazed and furious.

'I want to talk to the embassy,' I replied icily.

'You are free to do that,' said Fernández equally icily.

Cubana in 1969 was an unreliable airline and its flights were unpredictable, so I spent the next few days ostentatiously sulking in my room at the Habana Libre (ex-Habana Hilton) Hotel. In my calmer moments I was happy that I had not been accused of espionage.

When I got back to London I found the government had written to the *Financial Times* listing how I had gone about the island suggesting that it was in the grip of plagues.

A year or two later I was allowed back with a visiting British trade delegation and was allowed with them to shake the Comandante en Jefe's hand at a reception at the British embassy.

In 1975 I was invited back again with hundreds of bankers from round the world as an honoured guest at the celebrations of the twenty-fifth anniversary of the National Bank and once again shook Fidel Castro's hand. The occasion was a late night cabaret show staged for the bankers in the *Plaza de la Catedral*. As the dancers and singers beat their way through the programme under the lights of a stage set against the façade of the cathedral, western bankers, most of whom could not understand the revolutionary lyrics and would have heartily disagreed with them if they had understood, furiously applauded each succeeding turn in the warm Caribbean night. It was good for business.

Like all the other guests I was given a set of two silver *peso* commemorative coins in a cash of red plush and velvet. They lie in my study slightly tarnished now, the Cuban equivalent of those ornate parchments hung framed on the walls of houses in Ireland and other Catholic countries attesting to the fact that the Pope has been pleased to grant the householders a plenary indulgence.

The twentieth century architecture of Havana is unlikely ever to get the attention the earlier buildings are now enjoying, at least while Castro has any say. The last two years of the last century and most of this are not edifying objects of contemplation for a proud Cuban revolutionary. To restore twentieth-century architecture would run the risk of reminding Cubans of the degradation of the neo-colonialism of Spain.

Cuba, freed from Spanish rule by the intervention of the United States in 1898 became a nearly independent republic in 1902. In its early years until 1932 it was subject to the so-called Platt Amendment by which the government of the United States formally arrogated to itself the right to intervene in the affairs of the island.

One part of the island was to belong for ever to the United States. Guantánamo Bay in the far south-eastern corner of the island is among the finest and deepest in an island of fine, deep harbours. Semi-independent Cuba ceded the place to the United States in perpetuity.

The sight of a tropical equivalent of the Berlin Wall manned by the soldiers of two countries whose governments hated each other was, I convinced myself one self-indulgent day in Havana, so unutteraby exotic that it was not to be missed. I had to see on the ground the clash of Latin and Anglo-Saxon, of the imperial and the anti-imperialist, of Ariel and Caliban. And the visit there would be combined with that most delicious and instructive method of travel, an overnight train journey, one which in this case would take me the long snaky length of the island to Santiago, capital of the Oriente.

Friends and acquaintances in Havana, members of that incomprehensible worldwide conspiracy against train travel, warned against the Cuban railways. The trains, they said, were plagued by thieves. The accepted wisdom in the capital was that many of those who boarded in Havana never reached their destination but were horribly mangled in dreadful disasters on the line. Those males who embarked cleanshaven in Havana, if they survived, alighted in Santiago, they said, with long white beards.

The Cuban state itself seemed little more sanguine about the rail system. 'The Most Expensive Breakfast in the World', an award-winning short at that year's Havana Film Festival, told the true story of the driver of a shunting engine who so lusted after a tomato sandwich for breakfast that he left his locomotive switched on, allowing it to move off, career for miles and finally cause an expensive accident. I was not, however, to be put off.

Train Number One leaves the Havana Central Station every evening at ten minutes past six. It is due in Santiago, 860 kilometres away on the far side of the Sierra Maestra, the mountains in which Castro and his comrades started the war which was to overthrow Batista, thirteen and three-quarter hours later at five to eight in the morning. That is the theory: the practice, as I was to find out, is other.

Shortly before six o'clock one evening I boarded Train Number One and settled in my comfortable but dusty first-class seat in an air-conditioned open carriage beside a young man who was already asleep. It was drizzling and my spirits sank. The rain combined with the grime on the outside of the window to produce a film through which it was impossible to see clearly. Was the countryside going to go by in a disappointing muddy blur? Was there going to be no one to talk to?

As the train started, punctual to the second, the carriage was addressed by a very beautiful brunette in her late twenties.

'I am Marta, your *ferromoza*,' she said starting her short evening lecture on civics and the proper socialist attitude to travel by rail with a flirtatious giggle.

'Children must not be allowed to run up and down the aisle. Your seats, which are adjustable, have ashtrays in the armrests. Use them. When you brush your teeth tomorrow morning do it in the lavatories provided. The restaurant car is next door.' Sensing from long practice that her audience knew the difficulties of getting into stationary restaurants in Cuba without foreign currency, she added 'Tickets will be handed out for dinner and breakfast.'

Another giggle and she was gone.

Gloom returned.

By now Train Number One had come to a halt at Gas Works Junction, a piece of suburban wasteland such as can be viewed at some moment from every long distance train on earth. Marta was succeeded by two policemen who asked everyone which were their bags, presumably to frighten the more timorous thieves.

Things began to get better. The train picked up speed to fifty miles an hour across the green plain surrounding Havana. The speed and the evening sun dried the film of dirt on the windows allowing sight of neat carpets of sugar cane punctured every few miles by the tall smoking chimney of a *central* or sugar factory.

The man beside me awoke. He was a soldier who was serving in Havana but travelling back home to Camagüey, the cattle capital of Cuba a few hundred miles to the east. But he was also a member of the Cuban national cycling team and so did more time training for races than for battle.

Like me, he preferred train travel to going in some cramped bus. You were not boxed in, you could stretch your legs and have a meal.

It got dark quickly and the horizon glowed a beautiful red here and there where they were burning the cane fields to reduce the foliage and make the task of cutting the cane a lighter, though dirtier, job.

We were in the port of Matanzas by eight o'clock and as our diesel pulled us out of the station and away from the sea I thought of what Alberto Korda, the veteran Cuban photographer and underwater explorer, had told me in Havana about the treasure he had found at the bottom of the bay and how it came to be there.

In 1628 the Protestant Dutch made the greatest effort they

were ever to mount to break Catholic Spanish power in the Caribbean and South America. One Dutch fleet was sent to Brazil with the ludicrously unrealistic task of attempting to capture Potosí, the immensely rich silver mine in the Andes of Upper Peru.

Two fleets were sent to Cuba to intercept the convoys ferrying home the treasure to Spain from the New World. One of them under the famous admiral Piet Heyn, whose father had been enslaved in a Spanish galley, was stationed off the north coast of the island. Despite frantic attempts by the Cuban governor to warn him of the danger he faced in Cuban waters, Juan de Benavides sailed from the Mexican port of Veracruz with a convoy of treasure. On 5 September the two met, Heyn's more powerful fleet blocking Benavides' entry to Havana. The twenty-two Spanish ships ran for cover in Matanzas Bay but many were captured. Those which ran on the rocks were sacked by Heyn's men who brought back enough loot to allow their masters, the Dutch West India Company, to declare a fifty per cent dividend. The Spanish king Philip IV had lost 1,000,000 ducats in silver and three times that value in ships and guns. Losses by private merchants came to 6,000,000 ducats. It was a major disaster for Spain, rocking the throne, halting payments to the army fighting Heyn's compatriots in Flanders and plunging the fleet's home port, Seville, and Andalusia even deeper into economic depression. Benavides was put to death on his humiliating return.

But, according to Korda, among the vessels which went to the bottom there was still a fortune to be brought up. And there on the other side of the carriage was where it had all happened.

It was now time for supper. 'Sandwich or chicken?' said the woman from the restaurant car. 'Beer or soft drink?' Armed with the slips of paper she gave us our carriage filed down the aisle to the adjoining carriage with all the confidence of just souls on the day of judgement. We queued at a hatch where we were handed fat sandwiches, roughly wrapped in thick greaseproof paper, or big pieces of roast chicken and warm chips in plastic containers acquired from Cuban airlines. The drinks came in anonymous bottles. We paid our *pesos* at the checkout and sat satisfied and happy on stools at counters along the sides of the carriage, without benefit of knives and forks, gnawing and slurping. The chicken bones and paper went into cardboard boxes on the floor.

It was a far cry from the ordered atmosphere of *Wagons-Lits* in Europe but the enjoyment was the same.

Back in our seats we did not have to wait long for the dining-car staff to come round offering the strong sweet black coffee in tiny cones of brown paper for a few cents. The cycling soldier offered me some boiled sweets. My evening was made and I dozed off.

At about three o'clock we reached Camagüey. The soldier said goodbye and I went back to sleep. It must have been more than an hour later when I woke up to find we had not moved an inch. The locomotive which was due to take us the remainder of the way had broken down and a new one was on its way from Santiago. Sometime after four we were on our way eastward into the Sierra Maestra.

Breakfast was a sandwich and a soft drink as we lumbered cautiously through the Sierra. Having heard frequently over the years of the heroic revolutionary battles in the mountains, it was something of a disappointment to see how gentle the contours were. Outside the town of Mella there was another long delay, long enough to allow those of us who wanted to to get out on to the track, stroll about and watch the farmer carefully ploughing behind two slow oxen.

As we bowled downhill towards our destination I encountered a jolly group of *ferromozas* sitting with their foreman in an empty carriage. They explained to me banteringly how useless he was, while he warned me against ever having to supervise the work of a group of flighty women. The foreman added proudly that he had come from a long line of railway workers. The women seemed equally keen on their jobs. One said she had spent years in Czechoslovakia studying textile design but was now much happier away from the cold, stiff-necked city of Prague and Czechs' attitudes of patronizing racial superiority to Cubans. Seeing my camera they all wanted their photos taken.

At precisely half past ten we pulled into Santiago station exactly two hours, thirty-five minutes late.

The Oriente is a rougher, tougher, poorer part of Cuba than the flat lush land round Havana. It is a land of rock and cactus, not of palm trees and sugar cane. In the nineteenth century when virtually all Spain's empire in America had fallen away and only Cuba and Puerto Rico were left, the rich, slave-owning sugar growers of the west of Cuba were reluctant to risk their fortunes in a war of independence with Spain. The estate owners of the Oriente, Ignacio Agramonte and Francisco Manuel de Céspedes, who were later to become bourgeois nationalist heroes in the pantheon of a Leninist Cuba, had less to lose and were more radical.

With few roads and more difficult communication, the Oriente gave the advantage to the nationalist guerrilla bands who, in 1868, proclaimed an independent Cuba. They fought 100,000 Spanish troops for ten years but were in the end unable to defeat them.

Finally, and for its own ends, the United States intervened and in a few weeks in 1898 routed the Spaniards, put an end to their empire and consolidated its own. The final battle took place in the waters off Santiago.

At half past nine on the fine sunny morning of Sunday 3 July of that year, the Spanish commander, Admiral Pascual Cervera y Topete, steamed his ill-maintained fleet – which he had just navigated groggily across the Atlantic and for which the Spanish government could not afford to buy ammunition – out of the narrow entrance of the harbour of Santiago de Cuba. He was attempting to break the naval blockade imposed by an over-whelmingly powerful US fleet moored in a semicircle outside under the command of Admiral William Sampson.

It was the culmination of months of agony for a man who seemed to have had foreknowledge of his fate. A year before in Cadiz, when war with the United States seemed a distinct possibility, an acquaintance said to him that he looked likely to be given the command of the squadron in battle.

'In that case I shall accept, knowing however that I am going to a Trafalgar,' he replied.

Knowing how ill-trained the Spanish navy was, the admiral added that only the expenditure of 50,000 tons of coal on manoeuvres and the firing of 10,000 shells in gunnery practice could halt the disaster he foresaw.

The government had already lost the Philippines to the United States that year and was desperate to save some shred of military honour. It ordered him to the Cape Verde Islands. Fearing for the ships if he were sent across the Atlantic he made his position plain to the navy minister in Madrid. But there was no going back. Stopping to take on some coal in Curaçao he reached Santiago in the early morning of 19 May. Ten days later his ships, his flagship the *Infanta María Teresa*, the *Vizcaya*, the *Almirante Oquendo* and the *Cristóbal Colón*, all armoured cruisers, and the destroyers *Furor* and *Terror*, were bottled in the harbour of Santiago by a much more powerful US naval force waiting outside the narrow entrance to the port.

The city of Santiago itself was also under siege by land from the US army and the population was slowly starving to death. As horses disappeared off the streets of the city and into the stew-pots, Cervera, a skilled, respected and popular commander, fired off appeals for supplies.

On 22 June he appealed to the navy yard in Havana,

'Six-sevenths of the 5.5-inch ammunition is useless, the fuses not reliable, and we have no torpedos. These are the main deficiencies. If the government could send supplies so that they could arrive this week, it might still be time.'

Meanwhile there were not enough Spanish soldiers to maintain any proper defence of the city and his friend General Linares pleaded with him to order his men from their hammocks into his trenches. The same day as he appealed to Havana, Cervera cabled Madrid.

'As the question is going to be decided on land, I am going to send ashore the crew of the squadron as far as the rifles will go. The situation is very critical.'

The next day his cable to the navy ministry reported,

'I have disembarked crew to aid army. Yesterday five batta-lions went out from Manzanillo. If they arrive in time agony will be prolonged, but I doubt much whether they will save city.

As it is absolutely impossible for squadron to escape under these circumstances, I intend to resist as long as pos-sible and destroy ships as last extreme. Although others are responsible for this untenable position into which we were forced in spite of my opposition, it is very painful to be an actor therein.'

On 24 June he cabled Havana,

'With provisions we can hold out until end of July but I believe the siege will be over before then.'

A day later he told the Captain-General in Havana,

'I believe it my duty to set forth condition of squadron. Out of three thousand rounds for the 5.5-inch Hontoria guns only six hundred and twenty reliable; rest have been pronounced useless, and were not replaced by others for lack of stores before we left. Two 5.5-inch Hontoria guns of *Vizcaya* and one of *Oquendo* defective; they had been ordered to be changed for others. Majority of fuses not serviceable. We lack Bustamante torpedoes. *Colón* is without heavy armament. *Vizcaya* is badly fouled and has lost her speed. *Teresa* does not have landing guns, and those of *Vizcaya* and *Oquendo* are unserviceable. We have little coal; provisions enough for the month of July. Blockading fleet is four times superior; hence our sortie would be positively certain destruction.'

The same day he called Linares,

'I state most emphatically that I shall never be the one to decree the horrible and useless hecatomb which will be the only possible result of the sortie from here by main force, for I should consider myself responsible before God and history for the lives sacrificed on the alter of vanity, and not in the true defence of the country.'

From Havana at 10.45 p.m. on 1 July the Captain-General gave Cervera explicit instructions to sail out of Santiago.

One by one they emerged from the very narrow mouth of the harbour, already partially blocked by the *Merrimac*, a vessel the US sailors had sunk in the channel, at the foot of the crag on which was built the fortress of El Morro. Then they turned westwards in a dash for freedom. Each was destroyed, crippled by shellfire and rammed by its captain on to the beach. The *Furor* and the *Plutón* were gone well before an hour had passed. The *María Teresa* and the *Oquendo* by about ten-thirty. The *Vizcaya* by eleven o'clock.

As the USS *Texas* passed the stern of the *María Teresa* stuck on the rocks, her crew began to exult. Captain John Philip, the *Texas'* commander, seeing the horror of the burning Spanish ship shouted, 'Don't cheer. The poor devils are dying.'

Cristóbal Colón, the warship which some malicious fate had decreed should bear the name of the discoverer of America, made a run for it but was eventually overcome by the combined guns of *Oregon*, *Texas* and *Brooklyn* shortly before two o'clock. She beached herself and ran down her flag seventy-five miles to the west of Santiago.

In a battle which lasted less than four hours the US navy lost one man dead and one wounded. The Spaniards lost 350 of their 2,227 men dead, 160 wounded, 1,670 prisoner. They lost their fleet and in the waters off the Oriente they lost their empire. Under the US-Spanish peace treaty, to which the Cuban insurgents were not permitted to be a party, not only Cuba, but neighbouring Puerto Rico, the Philippines and Guam in the Pacific, were ceded by Spain into the hands of the United States or, briefly in the case of Guam, to the German Empire.

Captain Victor Concas, commander of the *María Teresa*, recalling the victory of Ferdinand and Isabella over the Moors in 1492 when Spain began to rise to greatness, later wrote,

'The bugle gave the signal for the start of the battle, an order which was repeated by a murmur of approbation from all those sailors and marines who were anxious to fight; for they did not know that those warlike echoes were the signal which hurled their country at the feet of the victor, since they were to deprive Spain of the only power still of value to her, without which a million soldiers could be of no service . . . The sound of my bugles was the last echo of those which history tells us were sounded at the capture of Granada. It was the signal that four centuries of grandeur were at an end and that Spain was becoming a nation of the fourth class.'

'We want them out of here.'

The Cuban major in the Frontier Guard Brigade helped me train the telescope on the gate in the fence miles away over which the Stars and Stripes still flew. This was the tropical Checkpoint Charlie. A dozen tiny figures ran from the yellow bus which had brought them to the fence to the checkpoint and into the Cuban bus which was waiting for them the other side. It was four o'clock on a blindingly hot afternoon and work at the US base was over for the day for those Cubans who still clocked on there.

Guantánamo Bay, an hour or so by road from Santiago, lay buzzing in the haze in a great natural amphitheatre of mountains twenty miles across. The hundred square miles of Guantánamo Bay is one of those superb, almost landlocked natural harbours surrounded by protective mountains which are to be found in the Caribbean and which offer seafarers some compensation for the cruel storms and hurricanes which sweep it. The base, 'Gitmo' to the US troops, is a rectangle of land and water which embraces the mouth of the bay and the two adjacent promontories. Vessels moving in and out of Guantánamo Bay have therefore to pass through waters controlled by United States forces.

With the major and a disagreeably arrogant young man from the local Communist Party as my guide and minder we had toiled up a long track in a Russian jeep to the eyrie at the top of the mountain. On each side of the track organ pipe cactuses stretched up their fleshy green trunks filled with water they had miraculously sucked from the rock. From time to time we passed a scrawny cowboy on a lean horse herding a few lean cattle. Goats somehow found a meal in the thorny bushes. There were iguanas the size of a strong man's arm. The flat carpets of sugar cane I had seen from the train might as well have been in another country.

From our vantage point, a post from which the Cuban army had been observing for thirty years, the forty-two square miles of the base were spread out distantly below us. The major pointed to US naval vessels at the docks and quays on the eastern promontary and across the bay on the western promontory to the airfield, firing ranges and a golf course. On the seaward side behind a hill bristling with antennae there was, he said, a bathing beach. Far away in the heat haze the lines of a large warship could be seen.

'A helicopter carrier,' said the major shortly.

At an early stage Fidel Castro decided that the continuing military presence of the United States on a corner of the motherland was an affront which was not to be tolerated. The annual cheque for rent of the base was refused and the United States government was left in no doubt that its troops were unwelcome. But while the nationalist point was clear and unequivocal the practical politics on the ground were more difficult.

The base provided many jobs in a region where there was not much employment. People from all over the Oriente came to Guantánamo to earn good money working for the *gringos*.

'Before the Revolution Caimanera was one big bar and brothel,' said the disagreeable young man primly.

The decision was taken to allow Cubans already working there to continue to work at the base and to continue selling the base water and power. At the same time the two villages of Boquerón and Caimanera were given special privileged treatment. Wages paid by the state in the area were a third higher than the average and the two villages were the first to be given colour television sets. The government tried to push up employment opportunities by reviving one of the world's most rudimentary industries by building saltpans on flat ground near Caimanera.

There was trouble in 1965 when Cuban fishermen were arrested and held as they sailed through US controlled waters. Castro cut off the supplies of Cuban power and water and since that day the Washington government had to produce its own electricity and procure water either from desalination plants on the base or via tankers bringing water from Puerto Rico.

Now the Guantánamo situation was being turned into a tourist attraction. Behind our lookout post the underground installations, which had presumably once housed an artillery command post, were being painted and spruced up and provided with maps and photographs which would instruct the visitor in the affront to Cuban national pride caused by the US presence on the soil of Cuba.

At the bottom of the mountain hard up against the wire was the fishing port of Boquerón. Why didn't we find some people who worked inside the base to talk to? I asked. With reluctance the disagreeable young man assented and we asked round the village.

'*Hay que bu'car a Dufu*,' said a villager.

Obediently we went in search of Dufu.

Dufu turned out to be Vincent Duffus, a tall, relaxed man with an easy smile sitting in the sun on the porch of his small house who had just retired from working at the base. He had been one of the many Jamaicans who had been taken on there because they spoke English. He was a living reminder of how, in the not too distant times of formal slavery, black labour used to be siphoned around the Caribbean as though it was one labour market. His easy manner and humanity seemed tacitly to ridicule the international ideological quarrel which kept the village where he lived fenced off from the military base where he had worked.

The major and the disagreeable young man were very unwilling to allow me to speak to him alone. But I did.

'I don' remember when I started to work at the base,' he said in a gentle Jamaican accent. 'It coulda been before the Revolution.'

Vincent's brother still worked at an office in the base and regularly brought out Vincent's pension for him in dollars. Despite the straightened circumstances in Cuba the elderly Jamaican seemed perfectly happy to end his days at Boquerón in the shadow of the base where had had worked for decades.

On the way back to the nondescript town of Guantánamo the disagreeable young man started to talk politics and I told him I was a member of the British Labour Party.

'Now the Labour Party, they tell me, is one of the less reactionary of the political parties in England,' he said. His remark recalled the succession of arch references to the 'bourgeois democracies' of Western Europe that I had heard in Havana in speeches and in conversations with the narrow members of the Party in Havana. His patronizing tone was no less insulting for being unthinking.

'The Labour Party was working for democracy in Britain for years before your Cuban Communist Party was thought of,' I replied with all the forcefulness I could muster in the heat. The rest of the journey was passed in silence.

It was not fanciful, I felt, to detect in the disagreeable young man's tone a not uncommon Cuban arrogance. This is an arrogance that may be compounded of centuries of Spanish imperial pride, native to the biggest island in the Caribbean. It is an arrogance compounded with the intellectual certainty given to those mean spirits whose horizons are bounded by a literal interpretation of Marxism-Leninism, an arrogance tested and tempered by the need to outface a powerful and implacable neighbour to the north. But I was not pleased.

Chapter Three

The North-East

'I say to them: 'Police, let go me sweet husband!' and with that I poke a rock in one of them . . . Then they let go a thing call teargas. That was something . . . My eyes burning me . . . I can't breathe . . . My head spinning and I can't see . . . It was like fire.'

Marina Harrigan quoted in *Anguilla's Battle for Freedom*, 1967 by Colville L. Petty and Nat Hodge.

'Where will you be staying?'
The question from the policewoman in the blue serge uniform was scarcely audible.
I told her.
'Have a nice stay,' she replied equally quietly. Or it might have been 'Have a nice day'.
I had come from San Juan in Puerto Rico where Hispanic declamation was wedded to US salesmanship in a society of noisy, careless, voluble ebullience. Anguilla, in contrast, was all understatement. Geographical understatement as much as verbal understatement.
The flight had been enchanted. After the jungles of Puerto Rico the little plane had bumped low across the north-east Caribbean past the British Virgin Islands, silhouetted to the north in the afternoon light. Their outlines certainly bore no resemblance to the martyred Hundred Thousand Companions of St Ursula after whom Columbus is supposed to have named them. Rather they lay like so many Gibraltars tossed carelessly by some Titan into the sea. What race of poets had given them their fantastical names? Fallen Jerusalem, Great Dog, Dead

Chest, Little Jost van Dyke, Virgin Gorda.

In the clear sunlight the presence of small, boldly-contoured islands in a sea like the Caribbean had the strange effect of heightening reality, re-emphasizing the nature of both land and sea. The quality of the land as a refuge for man from the perils of the sea became more accentuated as the islands reared up out of the water, invulnerable to any attack from the ocean; the immensity of the sea for its part was heightened by reference to the mere specks of land which it encompassed, a sense extended still further by the rain. The rain clouds never seemed to be able to encompass the sea from horizon to horizon; rain would often be seen falling on some stretch of the sea from some isolated bank of cloud and in all but the heaviest storms there was always somewhere where the skies were clear. Unlike the gloomy, comprehensive and semi-permanent cloud cover of northern Europe, isolated clouds came and went over the Caribbean, dropping their quota of rain in showers which quickly passed.

Later, the volcanic peak of Saba showed up hazily to the south, as if to contradict the sharp reality of land and water round the Virgin Islands. Distant and mysterious, Saba was a grey never-never land floating somewhere between sea and cloud.

Anguilla looked suburban in comparison, even workaday. From a distance the long flat island seemed no more than the westward breakwater to the glittering and cosmopolitan pirate isle of St Martin from whose heights a few miles away to the south-east across the Anguilla Channel the lights were beginning to twinkle. No mountains on Anguilla, no jungle, just scrubby vegetation and nondescript houses erected anywhere. British reserve after Spanish rhetoric.

Such a mixture is part of the Lilliputian charm of the north-eastern Caribbean. In a maximum of an hour's flight – in some cases in no more than a few minutes – you can go from a tropical Spanish culture like Puerto Rico's to a quiet British colony like Anguilla; from the peace of Dutch Saba – where very few of the inhabitants speak Dutch – to St Barthélemy ('St Barts'), now part of the French Republic, once Sweden's outpost in the Caribbean; from St Croix, a colony of the United States which within living memory was Danish, to the tiny monarchy of St Kitts and Nevis where 9,000 Nevisians labour night and day to keep at bay the hegemonic pretensions of 37,000 Kittitians. On St Martin, divided since the days of Louis XIV between two European powers, you can, as nowhere else in the world, walk over the border from France into the Kingdom of the Netherlands. The map of mediaeval Burgundy was never more complex; the local jealousies among the kingdoms, principalities and dukedoms of nineteenth-century Germany were never more bitter. Then there is Redonda where a black lawyer from the British colony of Montserrat set out his claim to rule over the uninhabited rock in the ocean whose king had always been taken to be an English literary agent living in Sussex. Did Byzantium ever have a more complex politico-dynastic dispute?

Not that the powers are too keen to be kept here. The Dutch have been trying unsuccessfully for years to work out a way to persuade their Caribbean fellow citizens on Saba and Statia to seek independence from the Netherlands. The French are happy enough to see the French *tricolore* floating in the Caribbean. But they also realize that it has cost billions of francs. Most importantly, it is clear in Paris that the French declaration that Guadeloupe, St Martin, and St Bart's are as inalienable parts of the French Republic as are the Boulevard Montparnasse or the vineyards of Nuits St Georges, has not brought a peaceful end to political debate in the French Caribbean. The United States, for its part, is keen to maintain a presence in the Caribbean but has its doubts about the wisdom of trying to absorb Spanish-speaking Puerto Rico as a full State of the English-speaking Union. Successive generations of British administrators have put their powerful minds to scheming how to get rid of the colonies now that they no longer produce wealth, but are places to be subsidized and defended, a source of international diplomatic embarrassment and, at times, ridicule.

But, like so many burdocks caught and tangled in the wool of elderly ewes, some of these scraps of islands in the north-eastern Caribbean have clung on to their metropolises. The Gullivers have been tied down fast with the gossamer ropes twisted by the peoples of Lilliput.

Drunk on such thoughts, I left the little airport, built with a simple modern elegance born of a tight budget and hard thinking by some government architect, for Lloyd's Guest House.

The journey by taxi confirmed the first impressions captured from the air. This was Caribbean Britain at its most reticent: no relics of empire even. No fortifications, no barracks, no great houses, no abandoned sugar mills. Just crocuses, banks of delicate yellow crocuses growing wild in every untidy field, along every road, in every scruffy garden.

Since the English arrived in 1650 there has never been very much to defend on Anguilla. The Anguillians never became rich when all they could produce for export was salt and when there was never enough fresh water for any crop to be cultivated.

Père Jean-Baptiste Labat, a French Dominican friar who in 1722 published a thrilling best seller on the West Indies, *Nouveau Voyage aux Iles de l'Amérique*, makes the comment that the Anguillians were so often raided by French corsairs that 'they in the end found safety only in the poverty to which the frequent visits of our people reduced them.' Once they made a little money from the sea-island cotton but the crop was destroyed by drought and the boll weevil. The only industry came from putting together the sun and sea water to produce salt in a few saltpans.

Lloyd's Guest House is one of those places whose friendliness comes as a welcome shock to travellers who have to endure the usually impersonal but always overpriced attention of the Fortes and the Sheratons. Vida Lloyd herself belongs to the race of innkeepers, who include the Cranstons on Saba and Miss Patterson of the St James Hotel in St George's, Grenada, who feel an urgent personal obligation to make their guests feel comfortable. Recognizing a hot, thirsty and tired traveller, she showed me a cool white bedroom with an enormous electric fan and served me an iced drink and a large plate of biscuits for which she never charged me.

The Guest House is an unpretentious family place, a one-storey building with a wide veranda, out of sight of the sea but with a good view of the cottage hospital. Its sitting room is full of comfortable armchairs, shaggy carpets and plastic tablecloths. The enormous television set is left permanently switched on. By the telephone is a photograph taken in Scotland of Queen Elizabeth II, with Prince Philip, both of them dressed in a kilt. On the wall beside the biblical texts hang pictures of Prince Charles and Lady Diana. Beside a pile of old magazines is a photograph of Mrs Lloyd's late husband David when he was a member of the government of St Kitts-Nevis-Anguilla, and a framed certificate of her qualification as a health visitor.

Dinner was at seven o'clock, served at a dining table loaded with bottles of Worcester Sauce and tomato ketchup, tins of instant coffee and evaporated milk, salt, pepper, mustard, sugar and most of the other additives mankind had ever invented to make food more palatable. All the indications were that the meal would be of greater human than culinary interest. And so it was.

A thin old white man of advanced years with a pustulated, scrofulous face was already at work on a plate of vegetables. He managed to combine extreme taciturnity with pronounced atrabiliousness. As the sound filtered over from the large television set behind him he snuffled and snorted his disgust at the doings of whatever politician featured on the news. He seemed to be a permanent guest and was the object of Mrs Lloyd's particular attention. I gathered he had been born in Jamaica and had spent his life working for some oil company in Trinidad.

We were soon joined by a jolly black man in his forties with a huge beard of biblical proportions who, like me, was soon tucking into large pieces of roast chicken. The old white man seemed reluctant to be sitting at the same table as him and was particularly reluctant to respond to his pleasantries. From the kitchen Mrs Lloyd sent her encouragement to eat up and ask for more.

The jolly bearded black man announced that he taught music. 'Where?' I asked.

'Oh, the Juillard in New York, Los Angeles, San Francisco, the US Virgin Islands, about fifty places. I like conducting and I play most of the instruments of the orchestra . . . I don't think you can conduct very well if you can't. I like Handel's *Brandenburg Concertos*. Tum, tum, tum, tiddle-tiddle, tum, tum, tum. You know.'

Bach's?' I queried.

'Oh yes. Bach's,' he said.

I did not know it at that moment, but I was lodging in a historic house. Lloyd's Guest House, and indeed the Lloyds themselves, had played an important historical role. It had a part in the Anguillian Revolution. The Revolution of 1967 against the power of St Kitts was a comic opera whose inspiration was to be found deep (and genuine) in the roots of this apparently characterless and submissive island. For centuries Anguilla stretched out its life in independent and libertarian poverty, its whites nearly as destitute as the blacks, too indigent and infertile an island to aspire to the pretensions of an Antigua or a St Kitts, never mind the aristocratic gentility of a Barbados. It was never coveted for more than a few days by its Dutch or French neighbours and it was never tied any other place than England.

Colonized from St Kitts in 1650 it seldom merited consideration in London where administrators lumped it in with neighbouring British islands and did their best to forget about it. But the Anguillians were not happy to be under the control of some other island. In 1824 they were demanding that,

'no measure relation to the island of Anguilla shall originate or be agitated in the House of Assembly of St Christopher except in the presence of the Representative of Anguilla.'

In 1871 they petitioned the Colonial Office to administer the island directly from Britain not leaving them at the mercy of 'the legislative body of St Christopher who are utter strangers to us, ignorant of the community, careless of their wants and therefore unequal to discharge the important duties of legislation for us.'

In 1958 they earnestly sought 'the dissolution of the present political and administrative association of Anguilla with St Kitts.'

In 1967 it became crystal clear that Britain was not only deaf to these pleas but serious about quitting the Caribbean as fast as it could. It was shutting and bolting the door on its colonial past and on overseas possessions which were no longer strategically important and a source of power and riches, but a drain on the British taxpayer. Anguilla was being left for St Kitts and Nevis to deal with in an autonomous 'associated state' of St Kitts-Nevis-Anguilla. The constitutional situation was exacerbated by personal and geographic factors. St Kitts, after all, was eighty miles away, beyond St Martin, beyond St Barts, beyond Statia.

Robert Bradshaw, leader of St Kitts, had made an admirable career as a trade union leader on his island, breaking the power of the absentee landlords of the sugar estates. He had been in advance of his time in working for Caribbean integration. He had become the finance minister of the short-lived West Indies

Federation. But he also was a florid man with a well cultivated handlebar moustache who was happiest when seen in public dressed in a tail coat with a wing collar and a rose in his button-hole. He was an admirer of the autocratic Forbes Burnham, the Guyanese leader and gave every impression of being imperiously and high-handedly contemptuous of Anguilla. Anguillians said he had threatened to turn the place into a desert and make them eat each other's bones. There was, too, a strange group of US citizens who rallied to the Anguillian side. One was a lawyer from Harvard who supported a constitution for the island based on 'Life, Liberty and Property, and the pursuit of Happiness' and another was a businessman who wanted to make the island a paradise for his sand and gravel company. In 1967 the Anguillians revolted.

The first skirmish in the liberation struggle was in February when a crowd broke up the beauty contest at the Valley Secondary School to select Miss Statehood. The government in St Kitts saw the contest as a vital political event. If the Anguillians could be tempted into choosing a Miss Statehood they might come round to accepting statehood itself. But that was not to be.

Cromwell Bowry, a Kittitian artiste had just begun his rendition of *My Grandfather's Clock* to a nervous audience when the fifty Anguillian freedom fighters went into action. They cut the electricity supply and rained stones and bottles on the zinc roof of the school. The contestants, Anne, Linda, Blondell, Edwena, Betty and Maycelle who had smelt trouble and who were reluctant participants in any case, fled as did Tunka Abdurama, the fire-eating magician, comedian and limbo dancer who had come from St Kitts with Cromwell Bowry to try and make the politically sensitive evening go with a swing. The police, loyal to Bradshaw, replied with tear gas and batons.

As the police counter-attacked the Anguillians, a young woman took flight across the adjoining cemetery and fell into a grave where Tunka was already hiding.

'Where am I?' she shouted.

'In heaven, darling,' he replied.

That anyway was Tunka's story.

The next day there was another fracas with the police which gave rise to Marina Harrigan's lament (see p. 59). The Anguillians even went as far as getting together with Bradshaw's political opponents on St Kitts to mount a cock-eyed invasion of that island. Unfortunately for them their landing craft, the good ship *Rambler*, a 35-foot sloop, had no compass. The seventeen-man invasion force arrived late on St Kitts, expecting half the island to be waiting to join them in the overthrow of Bradshaw, only to be greeted by a mere handful of Kittitians none too keen on taking up arms.

The invasion was a farcical failure but the Anguillians would *not* be put under Bradshaw and Kittitian rule. In a referendum of 6 February 1969 a unilateral declaration of independence and a republican constitution were approved by 1,739 votes to four and a month later several hundred British paratroopers, marines and metropolitan policemen arrived. Sensibly neither side fired a shot. Still the Anguillians would not bow to St Kitts. The British were obliged to govern the island from London and in 1980 they agreed wearily that the place could formally become a colony again. Lilliput had vanquished.

Vida Lloyd's husband David had worked in Bradshaw's Labour Party and when in 1967 the Anguillians started becoming violent towards anyone who stood for continuing links with St Kitts, Lloyd became a target. Six shots were fired at the Guest House on 20 April, and nine days later another six shots were fired at his garage damaging his car. The big attack came a month later. More than fifty rounds were put into the house but no one was injured.

Mrs Lloyd showed me where the bullet holes were still to be seen on the outside wall near the windows of the bedrooms where the Peace Corps volunteers were sleeping and she pointed to where the plaster and paint were covering the scars in the wall of the dining room. She complained that the attack came despite that fact that at the time her husband was not active in politics and that she, as a nurse, had always steered clear of affiliation.

'You can't treat patients if they think you're going to hurt them because you're a member of another party. You've got to have a pure heart for nursing.'

After more than two decades time had not yet healed the hurt of the attacks.

In the years since its revolution Anguilla has prospered hugely, but quietly, so that an island whose inhabitants once had to emigrate to find work now has more jobs than people to take them up.

The primitive salt industry has collapsed. At Sandy Ground, a village built on a spit of land between a shallow lagoon and the sea the remains of the industry lie abandoned in the sun. The punts that the Anguillians used to harvest the salt from the salt pans in the lagoon are holed and lie rotting in the water. On the quayside in front of the house of the Chief Minister, Emile Gumbs, are two whitish mounds each a hundred feet long and six feet high which seem to be composed of dirty snow. The last harvest of salt, hard and congealed, lies abandoned, gradually over the years dissolving back into the sea from which it came. The shed where the salt used to be crushed and put in bags is locked and deserted.

The rich and their money have found a haven in Anguilla, attracted by its quiet discretion and the fact that ultimate responsibility for the island lies with the British government. In the 1980s little banks catering to the tax evaders, the drug smugglers and the money launderers registered themselves in Anguilla. The majority of them did their business, scarcely taxed and unregulated, outside Anguilla. At one point there were forty-eight, or one for every 150 Anguillians. Pressure from London and Washington eventually forced most of them to close and the number was trimmed back to a dozen. The survivors do a roaring trade.

On the south-western tip of the island overlooking a silver beach is Coccoloba where the rich tourists stay, or, to quote the brochure, 'Where knowing travellers come to nest'. It is a series of green-roofed chalets grouped round a central building erected vaguely in the style favoured by the Emperor Nero. The brochure, illustrated by photographs of black servants and white guests, is suitably expensive looking and beguiling in the Madison Avenue manner given that a nest in the high season can cost £380 a night. Plus 10% service charge and 8% government tax.

Coccoloba

Unobtrusive service
anticipates, coddles,
and strives to please.

And the uncompromising
quality of a
truly
creative
kitchen
that daily
produces
a three-act potpourri
of culinary delights
to please the eye
and palate.

Though claims for culinary excellence in the English-speaking Caribbean must always be treated with suspicion, the place seemed friendly enough, a spot where tourists could come and buy expensive fantasies from willing sellers.

Government House is modest in comparison, a collection of bungalows and huts on a small rise a few hundred yards outside The Valley. Brian Canty the Governor, a middle-aged commonsensical official from the Foreign and Commonwealth Office, had spent a career in the East Indies, in Jamaica and then as Deputy Governor in Bermuda. He doubtless kept a white uniform and a helmet with ostrich feathers in a cupboard for special occasions but, not cast in the viceregal mould, no 'Foreign Office high-flier', he was clearly a man without great ceremonial pretensions. Ceremonial pretensions would in any case have clearly been out of place for the Governor of a colony as small as Anguilla.

We talked about the difficulties the island was facing as it became too prosperous to continue receiving the grants from the international aid agencies and how the problem had always been to get enough fresh water on Anguilla.

Then I turned the conversation to the death penalty. Some wretched Grenadian had killed his Grenadian girlfriend on Anguilla and had been convicted by a jury of murder. The death sentence was mandatory, even though Anguilla was a colony of a country where people were no longer hanged. The Anguillians were calling strongly for it to be carried out and so a man's life was in the hands of this unassuming official who was responsible for public order in an island which had already given London much too much trouble. If he took the awesome decision to allow him to hang it would haunt him. If he freed him he, might have riot and disorder on his hands. The choice clearly lay heavy on Brian Canty's shoulders.

The value placed on life on Anguilla had clearly risen since the days of slavery – even if, ironically, it was the blacks who were now demanding capital punishment and the whites who were demurring. The fact that Canty had to take an agonizing decision about the life of one murderer contrasted well with the state of casual massacre which was the rule among the Spanish speakers who lived around the rim of the Caribbean in Central America. And Anguillians, unlike the Mexicans or Guatemalans, have a humane record of staging their revolutions without anyone being killed. Happy the island whose inhabitants need fear nothing worse than a whiff of tear gas.

Père Labat visited the island of St Martin, across the channel from Anguilla, for a few days in 1705. It had been divided since 1648 between the French – who called their area Saint-Martin – and the Dutch – who called theirs Sint Maarten.

As soon as he arrived, the French Commandant told the schoolmaster to sound a conch shell to call the colonists together for worship. Labat said he was worn out by the way the inhabitants unceasingly importuned him to say mass, perform baptisms, teach the catechism, announce banns of marriage, perform weddings and hear their confessions.

'They hardly gave me time to finish my dinner before I had to get back to the church,' he grumbled. They were unwilling to see him depart.

The island slumbered on piously for centuries, divided between the two European powers and those few inhabitants who had any ambition of emigrating to the United States or to Curaçao and Aruba when the oil companies set up large refineries on those islands. A one-act comic opera was performed one Sunday afternoon in 1940 when, after the fall of the Netherlands to the Germans and before France surrendered, fourteen French troops from Saint-Martin marched into Philipsburg, hauled down the Dutch *tricolore* and hoisted the French one. The Dutch boys threw stones at them and they pulled back a fortnight later after France, too, had fallen.

Labat would not recognize the island today.

'Wine me, Dine me, 69 me,' say the T-shirts hung out to catch the tourist eye along Front Street in Philipsburg, the capital of Sint Maarten. 'Caution: I scream when I come'. There is clearly money to be made in helping visitors to the island to advertise their need for casual sex.

There are fast food joints along the potholed Front Street and the greater part of one shopping mall is taken up by the Coliseum 'casino' where, behind a couple of plaster Grecian columns, a hundred slot machines await the onset of the cruise passengers. In shops with names like Ram and Ashok listless Indian salesmen offer lurid jewellery and cheap electronic goods.

The street, the main shopping centre of the island, rings with the cries of New Yorkers – and some French – hunting for bargains in the sun.

Sint Maarten is one of the most repellent places in the Caribbean, a graceless monument to vulgarian greed, a charmless place which should be avoided by tourists and travellers alike. It is an island of about thirty-five square miles, studded with mountains bearing names like Pic du Paradis and Mont O'Reilly. This island as a whole is a free port; you present your travel document to the police as you arrive at the international airport on the Dutch side and you are then free to roam the whole island; there are no checks on the border between the two sides. Nor are there customs inspections when you arrive because no duty is levied on anything.

The tourist industry in Sint Maarten has made the Dutch side a sort of Atlantic City in the sun with virtually every beach, even those within yards of the end of the runway of the busy airport, thronged with garish 'resort hotels'. It was conjured up out of a quiet island by Claude Wathey, travel agent and the local political boss, who was first elected to political office in 1951 and who ran Sint Maarten for decades on the basis, as he freely admitted, of buying votes, of favouring his political friends and seeing off his political opponents.

When Fidel Castro's revolution in 1959 brought an end to the stream of US tourists to Cuba Wathey realized that Sint Maarten could benefit hugely. With determination and much hard work Wathey and his political friends pieced together a mass tourist industry, taking advantage, for instance, of the fact that casinos were legal in Sint Maarten and illegal in Saint-Martin. As the Wathey business empire grew he became ever richer and his political machine, the Democratic Party, ever more powerful, ever more capable of aiding those who supported him and doing down those who did not.

Tourism transformed the Dutch side producing an unplanned sprawl of unsightly buildings and a business boom which sucked in workers and traders from far and wide. In 1951 there were only 1,458 people in Sint Maarten, today there is a floating population of somewhere between 50,000 and 100,000 working on the Dutch side: immigrants from the other Dutch islands of Curaçao and Aruba, dogged, hard-working Haïtians doing the dirtiest jobs, Indian traders, housemaids and whores from the Dominican Republic, shop assistants and bellboys from Dominica, Lebanese businessmen, European accountants, retired people from the United States and Canada. The native population is now in a tiny minority in Sint Maarten, even discounting the tourists who arrive every year in their hundreds of thousands by jumbo jet from North America and Europe. The lack of customs controls, allied to the floating population of tourists and migrant workers, encouraged the massive import and use of drugs which in turn encouraged even more political corruption than there had been before.

Wathey maintains a relationship of mutual detestation with The Hague: when Queen Beatrix visited the island in 1987 Wathey chose the moment to be absent on a visit to Indonesia. He has even talked of Sint Maarten declaring independence though he knows that would be extremely difficult and bad for business. From time to time the Dutch, who have the responsibility of defending the Antillean territories, send a destroyer to patrol round the islands and when there is a unit of Dutch marines in Sint Maarten they patrol ostentatiously at the airport, shaven-headed, in uniform, rifles at the ready.

The French side is more closely linked to France than the Dutch side is to the Netherlands. French Saint-Martin is a *commune* of the *département* of Guadeloupe and thus by a stretch of Gallic imagination a part of France proper; Dutch Sint Maarten is merely a part of the Dutch Antilles and thus not considered part of the Netherlands. In fact it makes little difference to the poisonous atmosphere which prevails on both sides of the

Franco-Dutch border. On the French side, controlled by a *sous-prefet*, there is no problem with undesirable local politicians such as the Dutch have with the egregious Wathey. In Saint-Martin the problem is the metropolitan French. Lured by tax concessions which allowed them to offset against their income whatever moneys they invested in this distant *commune*, they have fallen on French Saint-Martin with all the rapacity of Wathey's *protégé* on the Dutch side. The native inhabitants live in a state of suppressed anger made all the worse by the customs men Paris has sent to try and control the cocaine trade.

Back on the Dutch side in Cyrus Watheyplein, the little square in the centre of Philipsburg named after Claude Wathey's father, I hailed a cab for the airport. A mountainous black taxi driver sulkily put her red-painted toe on the accelerator and we were off to the airport and the flight away from Saint-Martin. As we arrived I offered her a ten-dollar bill.

'Eight dollars. You got no change?'

I did not argue. Seldom were ten dollars better spent.

Eighty miles away Anguilla's erstwhile masters opted under British encouragement to take their country into independence in 1983. The two islands of St Christopher – St Kitts as it is usually known – and Nevis became a small monarchy owing allegiance, like its neighbours Jamaica, Antigua, St Lucia, Barbados, St Vincent and Grenada, to the Queen of England but effectively controlled by a small black political class through a parliamentary system. It had its own ambassadors and high commissioners – though not very many of them because they were expensive to maintain – and a seat at the United Nations and there was seldom a glance back to Anguilla. When Robert Bradshaw died, his Labour Party lost its parliamentary majority to a new conservative pro-business party and went into opposition.

St Kitts with its 37,000 people is a metropolis compared with Anguilla. Few islands could be more dissimilar. In place of Anguilla's low scrubby hills are St Kitts' jungle-covered peaks; in place of Anguilla's few untidy fields, long abandoned to the goats, are St Kitts' neat fields of sugar cane; in place of Anguilla's beaches of golden sand are the stretches of black volcanic sand; where Anguilla has no historic buildings – almost no buildings of note – St Kitts has great monuments to the past.

The weight of history lies heavy on St Kitts. Perhaps it was in-evitable that the leaders of this old island, formed, shaped and welded in slavery and in the bloody imperialist and colonialist struggles between France and England, would fall out seriously with the devil-may-care libertarians of Anguilla.

The island was discovered by Columbus on 12 November 1493 but not subsequently settled by the Spaniards. Settlement came when Captain Thomas Warner arrived in 1624 and found a few Frenchmen already established. Three years later the island's sixty-eight square miles were peaceably divided between France and England, the former having the two ends and the latter the middle. By mid-century a boom in sugar had started and the *entente cordiale* continually broke down as the island prospered.

Père Labat who visited the island in 1700 when it was still divided between the French and the English found the level of civilization so high and the inhabitants so civil, that, he said 'one would have been hard put to find more politeness in the best Cities of Europe'. The popular belief was, he recounted, that the nobility was on St Christopher, the bourgeois on Guadeloupe, the soldiers on Martinique and the peasants on Grenada.

Though he was a friar, he had an eye for women's fashion on the island and a well developed French conviction of the super-iority of Parisian *haute couture*.

> 'The English women are dressed in the French fashion, at least their outfits are very similar. These outfits are rich and magnificent, & would be of great good taste, if the women did not add things of their own; but as they always want to improve on the fashions which arrive from France, these extras upset all the symmetry & the good taste there would otherwise be. I have never seen so many gold, silver and silk tassels as there were on these women; they seemed covered from head to foot in them.'

Those directly responsible for such magnificence had a harder life. In his time as a slave in the eighteenth century Olaudah Equiano had occasion to get to know St Kitts shortly after he left the Slave Coast. The conditions in Jamaica were replicated on the island.

'It was', he wrote 'very common in several of the islands,

particularly in St. Kitt's for the slaves to be branded with the initial letters of their master's name, and a load of heavy iron hooks hung about their necks. Indeed on the most trivial occasion they were loaded with chains, and often instruments of torture were added. The iron muzzle, thumbscrews, &c. are so well known as not to need a description, and were sometimes applied for the slightest faults. I have seen a negro beaten till some of his bones were broken, for only letting a pot boil over. It is not uncommon, after a flogging, to make slaves go on their knees and thank their owners, and pray, or rather say, "God bless you". I have often asked many of the men slaves (who used to go several miles to their wives, and late in the night, after having been wearied with a hard day's labour) why they went so far for wives, and did not take them of their own master's negrowomen, and particularly those who lived together as household slaves. Their answers have ever been – "because when the master or mistress choose to punish the women, they make the husbands flog their own wives, and that we could not bear to do." Is it surprising such usage should drive the poor creatures to despair, and make them seek a refuge in death, from those evils which render their lives intolerable?'

The principal monument to colonial days is the huge fort of Brimstone Hill, the Gibraltar of the Caribbean, built on an outcrop of rock a few miles along the coast from Basseterre. Its bastions and barracks, magazines and colonnades, make it one of the most ambitious fortifications built anywhere in the Caribbean. That the fortress, which last saw a British garrison in 1853, is being preserved and appreciated as an architectural gem is to the credit of one Kittitian businessman, Lloyd Matheson, who has devoted half a life to Brimstone Hill. When I first went to St Kitts in the late 1960s he and a small band of helpers were laboriously trying to clear the site and cadge money from whatever source seemed likely. Twenty years later Matheson, retired now but still as fanatically devoted to the old building, had set up a small museum on the site and in his study, hung with antique maps of the island, discussed with me his chances of persuading the French government to send a naval detachment to take part in a pageant on the Hill.

Today, free of slavery, free of the absentee planters, free of control from London, unworried by wars between the French and the British, the people of St Kitts can go about running their own country as they like. They do it with competence. Unlike Sint Maarten or Antigua, for instance, they have preserved a sugar industry and thus saved the island from too great a dependence on tourism. What mass tourism there is in St Kitts is cleverly confined to a 'resort hotel' and 'development' which seems to have little to do with the life of the rest of the island.

Political control of the island has been in the hands of moderate conservatives or a cautious labour party which, like the British one, always owed more to Methodism than to Marxism. In 1980, after Labour had been in office for three decades, the conservative People's Action Movement pulled ahead in the elections. PAM's leader, Kennedy Simmonds, cut a deal with the Nevis Reformation Party from the sister island to put an end to thirty years of rule by Robert Bradshaw's Labour Party. The deal ensured that when independence arrived the 9,000 Nevisians would have a large amount of autonomy from St Kitts. Nevis can declare independence after having given the larger island six months' notice. The coalition of conservative Kittitians and Nevisians wobbled along for more than a decade.

Thousands in St Kitts, however, still revere the memory of the late Robert Llewellyn Bradshaw, the poor boy who went to work at sixteen in the sugar factory but who rose to become the most powerful in the land. He is revered less for what he did on Anguilla, more for his efforts to organize working people, and for his victory over the planters after a thirteen-week strike in 1948.

It was a happy, good-natured crowd which gathered in Basseterre to parade with music and banners round the streets of the town in commemoration of the trade union's half-century of existence. Along Fort Street they went in their red T-shirts, past the Treasury Building with its silver dome, past the ornate Victoriana of the Berkeley Memorial drinking fountain and clock in the middle of the Circus, through the colonial Regency elegance of Independence Square, past St George's Anglican Church. The band tootled indefatigably as grave policemen held up what little traffic there was. The march was led by a lady with a big straw hat and a strong voice with which she tempted the waverers out of the houses along the route.

'You are the people,' she intoned,
'The people are you.'
'Join our march to celebrate fifty glorious years of the St
Kitts-Nevis Labour Union.'
'You are the people,'
'The people are you.'

Enough obeyed her to make the parade a success. After all the
walking in the hot sun the procession broke up for picnics, at the
Old Grammar School Pasture from which the unwilling goats
had been chased. If Bradshaw was reviled in Anguilla he was still
being honoured in St Kitts.

'I underestimated Statia when I arrived,' said Christopher
Glover with a tinge of remorse about a clear case of bad judgement.

Gravely and courteously the old black man had offered his
services to me at the little airport of Sint Eustatius, grandly
named after Franklin Delano Roosevelt; slowly and carefully we
were driving towards Oranjestad in his ancient car. A very long
time ago, Christopher Glover informed me, he had quit his
home in St Kitts and life under the British flag, and arrived as an
immigrant to the Dutch queen's territory. He had not had to
bring his skills as a mechanic far; St Kitts loomed there a few
miles across the silver sea to the south. But now he was content.

'It's a quiet place,' he said.

A goat looked up and went back to cropping the grass on the
airport runway.

'There's no violence, no crime.'

'I can understand,' I said.

Silence.

A donkey on the road peered at us.

We motored cautiously another few hundred yards.

'That's The Quill,' he said pointing past the cactus to a
bracken-covered mountain, an extinct volcano which rose 2,000
feet to our left.

We progressed circumspectly on towards Oranjestad and he
dropped me off in the centre of the village.

The atmosphere of Oranjestad is that of a sleepy Devon village in a good summer. A hot sun, some ancient ruins, a handful of cars on the street, a church shielded by a few trees and a little supermarket where you can buy the essentials of European life, the newspapers and a few souvenirs. Perched on a low cliff it looks over the blue sea and the distant cone of Saba on the northern horizon. At the foot of the cliff beside the water's edge lies a peaceful promenade. It is all very quiet.

Except, that was, until a crocodile of black infants from the Governor de Graaff school came into sight. Hand in hand, two by two, they laughed, chirruped, giggled and, wriggled, the very quintessence of innocence, under the kindly eye of their teacher, each of them bearing a cardboard badge with the letters WFD. Dennis Sprott was delighted to see someone from London and invited me back to the school. Sprott was a committed admirer of the Church Army and had several times been to Dundee on Church Army business. As far as the badges were concerned, he explained it was the United Nations' World Food Day and that he had taken them down to the jetty so they would know where the fish they ate came from.

So there was some young life on Statia.

In Wilhelminaweg I wandered into a little picture gallery, the Park Place, and met Barbara Lane, the owner, who had moved down from the United States.

'It's wholesome here,' she said. 'There's no pre-frozen stuff. I bake my own bread and make my own sauces and jams and sherberts.'

Along the Synagogepad I looked at the eighteenth-century ruins of the Honen Dalim synagogue whose roof had fallen in long before the last Jew on Statia died in 1846. Along Kerkweg I gazed at the ruined Dutch reformed church which was consecrated in 1755 and which had had no minister since 1792.

Lieutenant-Governor George Sleeswijk received me in his gubernatorial bungalow. We sat on a sofa under a portrait of Queen Juliana.

'This is a quiet, conservative island, deeply loyal to the queen,' he said. 'We don't want mass tourism, just people

77

who can appreciate nature and the history of Statia.'

Wordlessly he expressed his distaste as I mentioned the raucousness of Sint Maarten.

He gave me his card. We considered whether the Dutch title of his superior *'Gouverneur'* who lived in Curaçao and had authority over several Dutch islands might better be translated into English as 'Governor General'. In that case his own title *'Gezaghebber'* or 'holder of authority' might better be rendered into English as 'Governor'. His status, he pointed out, was considerably higher than that of a lieutenant-governor of a state of the United States.

Because Statia, as the colony is universally known, is eight square kilometres in area and has only 1,600 people, this does not make questions of protocol any the less important. It was, after all, a question of protocol and the connection with the United States which brought Statia low all those years ago. In the eighteenth century it was Statia which was the raucous one and Sint Maarten which was the backwater. Before Rodney came.

Before Admiral Rodney, commander of the West Indies station came Statia was a thriving, ebullient bazaar of a place. Janet Schaw, an Edinburgh woman who wrote an account of her journeys under the pen name 'A Lady of Quality', came to Statia on 19 January 1775. She reported on her shopping experiences with all the enthusiasm of a modern traveller who had found a particularly good duty-free airport.

'From one end of the town of Eustatia,' she wrote, 'to the other is a continued mart, where goods of the most different uses and qualities are displayed before the shop doors. Here hang rich embroideries, painted silks, flowered Muslins, with all the Manufactures of the Indies. Just by hand Sailor's Jackets, trousers, shoes, hats etc. Next stall contains most exquisite silver plate, the most beautiful indeed I ever saw, and close by these iron-pots, kettles and shovels. Perhaps the next presents you with French and English Millinery-wares. But it were endless to enumerate the variety of merchandise in such a place, for in every store you find every thing, be their qualities ever so opposite. I bought a quantity of excellent French gloves fourteen pence a pair, also English thread-stockings cheaper than I could buy them at home. I was indeed surprised to find that the case with most of the British manufacturers, but I am told the merchants who export them have a large drawback . . . We purchased excellent claret for less than two shillings a bottle, and Portuguese wines of different kinds very cheap.'

The island which was first settled by the Dutch in 1636 had built up a very profitable entrepot business, as Sint Maarten was to do more than three centuries later. It had no very good harbour but it did have a very capacious roadstead where ships could be easily serviced by lighter. It also had a careenage where ships could be pulled out of the water and have barnacles and other encrustations scraped from their hulls.

The island was a Dutch possession but it did change hands with remarkable frequency. Between 23 July 1665 and 1 February 1816 it was bounced around as the possession of three countries as though they were playing 'Pass the Parcel' at some children's birthday party. It was initially Dutch, then came the English, who lost it to the French, then came the Dutch, then the English, then the Dutch once more, the French for a second time, then back to the English, next the Dutch for a fourth time, then the English for nine months, the French once more, later the Dutch, the French for a last time, then the English for the next to last time, the Dutch for a further three months, then the English, and finally the Dutch for good.

Sint Eustatius was within easy reach of British islands like St Kitts and Antigua, Spanish Cuba and Puerto Rico, the Danish Virgin Islands and French strongholds such as Guadeloupe and St Lucia. When these empires were at war with one another trade could often be done in neutral Statia with the Dutch who seemed to have absorbed the arts of commerce with their mothers' milk. For much of the eighteenth century the most profitable merchandise was slaves. Several thousand were bought and sold every year and quarters were built to hold 450 at any one time.

But Statia's boom time came when the American colonies revolted. The island, which had been declared a free port in 1756, became an important source of supply for the rebels, and the island merchants, many of whom were British, grew rich on the trade in gunpowder and weapons. The Dutch West India Company, under pressure from Britain, tried to impose a six month ban on the arms trade with the rebels in 1775 but the Statian merchants ignored the orders from Amsterdam. They took no notice when the ban was extended for a further year. The roadstead became a forest of masts with eighty ships riding at anchor at any one time. The ships brought in so great a quantity of goods that even though warehouses were continuously being built there was never enough space. Sometimes the warehouses were so full that the doors could be used no longer and goods had to be lowered down through holes in the roof. The Dutch also introduced their expertise in reclaiming land from the sea on which they could build new warehouses, but merchandise still had to be left out in the open air or under tarpaulins.

Time and again the British complained to The Hague about the trading practices of the Statians. British anger boiled over when the government in London learned what happened at Oranjestad on 16 November 1776. The small two-masted brigantine flying the new red and white striped flag of the Continental Congress of the United States of America arrived in the roadstead and saluted the Dutch flag. The *Andrew Doria* was a converted merchantman, one of the first four ships to be commissioned into the Continental Navy the previous year. She had sailed from the little port of Gloucester in New Jersey across the Delaware River from Philadelphia under the command of Captain Isaiah Robinson with orders from the Congress to pick up military supplies. Robinson was also to deliver a copy of the Declaration of Independence to Johannes de Graaff, the governor of the island.

In what was to be the first acknowledgment of the independence of the United States of America the Guns of Fort Oranje returned her salute. De Graaff was later to testify that it was a routine gesture but Abraham Ravene, Fort Oranje's commander, swore that the governor had prompted him to give the order to fire a salute even though he had not wanted to. De Graaff, the merchants and the 8,000 Statians were happy figuring the gesture could be good for business.

Admiral Sir James Young, commander of the Leeward Station at English Harbour in Antigua, was apoplectic and complained to de Graaff that, 'the colours and forts of the States General have been so far debased as to return the salute of these pirates and rebels and giving all manner of assistance of arms and ammunition and whatever else may enable them to annoy and disturb the trade of His Britannic Majesty's loyal and faithful subjects, and even the Governor of St Eustatius daily suffers privateers to be manned and armed and fitted in their port.'

The governor was recalled to The Hague for questioning but was confirmed in his post and returned to Statia in 1779. On 20 December 1780 Britain declared war on the United Provinces of the Netherlands. It was to bring the Republic low and it almost led to the annihilation of Sint Eustatius. On 27 January 1781 Admiral Sir George Brydges Rodney received orders from London to attack and subdue all the Dutch possessions he could in the West Indies paying particular attention to Sint Eustatius and Sint Maarten.

By 3 February his fifteen ships, able to disembark 3,000 troops were off Oranjestad. De Graaff was presented with an ultimatum; surrender within the hour or face destruction. The Dutch had not lavished money on defence. There was only one Dutch warship in the harbour and the garrison of Fort Oranje was of no more than fifty men and only five of the twenty-five cannon worked. The storage for gunpowder was so damp that the explosive had to be dried before it was used. Fort de Windt, according to the report made a few months previously by a visiting officer, had four cannon and a garrison made up of the constable, a small boy and a black maid. The masonry was so precarious that that year the parapet fell away when the guns were fired one morning. After firing two rounds for honour's sake, de Graaff surrendered Statia at about 3.30 p.m. Fort Oranje quickly became Fort George and was given a garrison of 650 men.

One hundred and thirty merchant ships fell at one blow to Rodney's force and the Admiral kept the Dutch flag flying for a month so that many more unsuspecting vessels were taken. The British set to plundering the warehouses that Mrs Schaw had so admired six years before. On 18 February all goods were confiscated. The doors of the warehouses were sealed and the contents prepared for auction. Rodney took particular care to strip the Jews, whom he deported, and the British merchants whom he considered traitors.

The joy caused by the news in London knew no bounds. 'It is reported that you are to be made a peer,' wrote Lady Rodney.

At the end of March Rodney sent back to England a convoy of thirty-four merchantmen crammed with £5,000,000 worth of plunder with an escort of warships under Admiral Hotham. It was not a successful operation. Admiral La Motte Piquet with a stronger force sailed from Brest, sighting the convoy off the Scilly Isles. Hotham told his convoy to scatter but the French nevertheless captured twenty-two of the merchantmen. Rodney, who was deeply in debt had been looking forward to his £150,000 share of the spoils, which would have paid off his gambling debts or financed more nights at the table. He was understandably mortified when most of that was lost.

The West Indian traders in London howled at Rodney's conduct during the capture of Statia and the matter was hotly debated in parliament. The affair was allowed to drop only after he had bolstered the British position in the Caribbean by crushing the French fleet at the Battle of the Saints the following year.

And what the Dutch lost to the British, the French were not long in seizing for themselves. As they did so they played out another scene in the millenial battle between England and Ireland. The *Connecticut Gazette and Universal Intelligencer* of New London in its issue of 25 January 1782 reprinted an account of the British defeat which had appeared the previous month in the Martinique *Gazette*. The French forces under the command of the Marquis de Bouille included several hundred Irish troops of the regiment of Walsh commanded by Count Arthur Dillon. In difficult weather a third of the total force of 1,500 landed early in the morning of 26 November 1781 at Jenkins Bay near the northern tip of the island. Without the British noticing, they pushed towards Fort Oranje. When they were eventually seen, the red Irish uniforms led the unwary defenders to think they were British.

'Count Dillon,' the newspaper continued, 'reached the barracks at six o'clock in the morning, and found a part of the garrison exercising on the parade. The enemy, imposed upon by the uniform of the Irish brigade, were soon undeceived by a fire from the latter within pistol shot. Governor Cockburne, on his way to the parade, was taken prisoner at the same time, by the Chevalieur (sic) Oconner, Captain of the *chasseurs* of Walsh. The Chevalieur Fresne pushed on to the fort, into which the enemy were throwing themselves in great numbers; he reached the drawbridge at the moment they were intending to raise it; Mons de la Motte; second Captain of the *chasseurs* of Auxerrois, rushed forward on the bridge, and by a well timed well directed fire, obliged the enemy to let go the chains. This vigorous attack, deserving the greatest encomiums, was the signal of victory.'

A few years later Dillon recalled that many of the troops who had fought under the British flag were in fact Irish Catholics and when they saw the opportunity of joining their compatriots fighting for the French against the English, they seized it.

'. . . on a single occasion,' he wrote, 'above 350 Irish Catholics, made prisoners at St. Eustache in the 13th and 15th English regiments, enlisted themselves into those of Dillon and Walsh, in which the greatest part of them exist still. Each soldier thus gained for France is worth 3 men to her; she has an enemy the less, a defender the more, and the blood of a citizen saved.'

Lieutenant-Colonel Thomas Fitz-Maurice of the Irish brigade was made governor of Statia. O'Connor, who took Cockburne prisoner, covered himself with glory in Statia.

The action on the island was to be one of the last actions of the Irish brigade of the French army. It had been in the service of France since the defeat of the Catholic Irish Jacobite forces at the hands of Protestant William of Orange in Ireland at the battles of the Boyne and Aughrim and the subsequent Treaty of Limerick of 1691. After those defeats many of the Jacobite forces went into exile in France and formed the brigade.

The revolutionaries had no use for it, as O'Connor's subsequent fate demonstrated. At the outbreak of the French Revolution, now promoted to major, the father of ten children and evidently a convinced monarchist, he was assassinated by republicans while trying to flee Guadeloupe.

Back in Dutch hands, the traders had one last Indian summer. In the closing years of the eighteenth century the island supported a newspaper, the Sint Eustatius *Gazette*, most of whose text was in English with some in Dutch. It was handsomely 'Printed by Benjamin Watson at the New Path where all manner of Printing is done with care and dispatch'. The advertisements it contained give clues to the sort of elegant slave-based life that was being lived on the island.

A Second Hand
HARPSICHORD
(Made by Kirkman)
to be sold reasonable.
Enquire of the Printer
St Eustatius, June 1793

or

FOR SALE
reasonable for Cash
A Few dozen of excel
lent Port Wine

or

For Sale
A black woman
named Can
dice and her Child. For
particulars enquire of
Will. Chadwick
St Eustatius October 10 1794

One notice records,

On Monday last departed this life, Mr Solomon Solomons,
a Gentleman of the Hebrew Nation,
Aged 30 years

He was True to his religious tenets, without Enthusiasm. –
To his Parent a dutiful son. – To his Sister an affectionate
Brother – and to his Wife a fond Husband. He was by
nature blest with a disposition for practising those virtues
which CHARACTERISE the GOOD MAN. His faith was in the
law of his Forefathers, he lived with TEMPERANCE, was
guided by PRUDENCE, and CHARITY was his constant companion; in all his Mercantile dealing JUSTICE presided,
and, when visited by a painful and lingering illness, his
FORTITUDE was truly conspicuous; and his last moment
evinced that his HOPE was in GOD.

France, which had captured the Netherlands and set up the pup-
pet Batavian Republic, was back again in 1795. The French
forced the Statians to pay the costs of the garrison and a monthly
indemnity of 8,000 Spanish florins. This, even more than Rodney's operation, impoverished the island and caused an emigration whose effects are still being felt. When an independent
United States became strong enough to trade directly with
whomever it wanted, Statia's entrepot function and the days of
her prosperity were over for ever.

The nineteenth century, and much of the twentieth, was a
time of decline. With the introduction of sugar beet in Europe
Statia suffered the competition that all West Indian sugar pro-
ducers suffered. When the Dutch finally emancipated their
slaves in 1863 agriculture all but petered out. But even in the
days of slavery it had been hard to get any crop, tobacco, sugar,
coffee or cotton, to grow satisfactorily. There were half-hearted
attempts to start other enterprises, growing sisal and cotton or
mining gypsum. But there were too few able-bodied people and
too few markets for these to succeed. The death of the last Jew
extinguished a line which had brought commercial flair to Statia
in the golden days. In 1939, the men of working age having emigrated, there were few males left, save the very young and the
very old. The 1,000 inhabitants who remained were huddled in
Oranjestad leaving the rest of the island deserted.

'You bin to Havana?' Pompier asked me as we waited at the
counter for the cook to finish preparing our meal in the dingy
Chinese restaurant.

Pompier had been among those who, despairing of finding work on his island, had taken to the sea. He showed me with pride the badge and certificate Esso had given him for his long service as second cook aboard their tankers. For years he had shuttled around the Caribbean helping to carry cargoes from the refineries on Aruba, the Dutch island in the south. But now he was home with a pension and with all the time in the world to remember the past.

'Very nice place Havana. We went there once. Very pretty girls. You could go to a house in Havana and they'd line up like soldiers.

'You could choose whichever you wanted. For fourteen dollars she'd go with you for the whole night.'

A long pause.

'Only fourteen dollars! Fourteen!'

Too old now to need the services of whores, Pompier lived out his declining years sailing over his glass of Heineken, a bowl of chop suey and the remembrance of long dead virility.

Half a dozen whites labour to keep a small hotel and a scuba diving business going in the face of adamantine Statian apathy. It is an uphill job. 'This is an island for travellers not for tourists,' said one of them. 'There's not the breeding stock to keep a tourist business going here.'

One or two sloppy guest houses make a little money catering to the Dutch. They arrive on package tours from the Netherlands in the hope they will pass their driving test on the deserted roads of Statia more easily than on the busy streets of Amsterdam or The Hague.

A small run-down hotel lies beside a long beach at the far end of a muddy track. A fierce Alsatian on a strong chain stands in the entrance defying all but the bravest visitor to enter.

A hopelessness hangs over Statia. How long would it be, I asked myself, before the energetic, innocent gaiety of Dennis Sprott and his children was swallowed up in the moody sectarian rancour of Statia's rival Christian denominations in the political pettinesses of a tiny island?

Like Pompier, Statia itself, a shabby and none too proud old bankrupt sitting in the sun, half-heartedly coaxes genteel tourists to visit the ruins of the former glories. But most Statians don't really care if they never come.

'En ze name off the Faazer and off ze Sonn and off ze Holy Spu-rut . . .'

In the Sacred Heart church one had to strain hard to catch the meaning of Father Janssen's English but the occasion was splendid. The candles on the altar gleamed, the congregation, predominantly black and dressed in their best, were hushed, the altar boys had scurried about with their tapers, the organist at her electronic keyboard had stopped her reverent musical doodles and the bride had finally arrived.

It was splendid but we all felt detached, cut off somehow. We sat cosily in the little church built of blue-grey volcanic stone, the church nestled snugly in the middle of the village which itself was protected by walls of rock from the world outside. The whole island, the precipitous top of some primeval volcano no more than five square miles in area, seemed no bigger than a glorified lifeboat in the middle of the Caribbean Sea.

This was one of the grandest events of the year in The Bottom, the island capital of Saba, a sliver of Dutch Ruritania in the Caribbean.

I had arrived on Saba two hours before.

'Would you mind shoving your immigration form in that milk churn behind you as you leave Saba,' said the immigration officer as he stamped my passport.

I said I would do.

The immigration stamp was florid and artistic like those postage stamps bearing all the major works of Titian which very small countries like the United Arab Emirates issue. 'Saba Unspoiled Queen', said the stamp around a silhouette of the island. There was a box for '*In*' and another for '*Uit*' perhaps to remind you that you had been in one of Her Netherlandish Majesty's possessions.

Not that Dutch has been widely spoken on Saba for centuries. When the island became Dutch definitively in 1816 it was stipulated that 'all government documents and regulations shall be translated into the English language as there is no one on this island who understands Dutch.'

The immigration officer's quiet and relaxed informality was very welcome after the terrifying landing.

To land on an aircraft carrier cannot be more exciting than arriving by air on Saba a few miles to the north of Statia.

Juancho Yrausquin airport is a ledge of volcanic lava on the edge of a mountain which rises up nearly 900 metres from the Caribbean Sea. On the tiny short runway which takes only very small planes there is a wall of solidified lava on one side and on the other water half a mile deep which foams and boils. At the far end, thankfully not visible to the passenger as he lands, arc rocks set in rows, each rock triangular like the tooth of some monster shark.

The little twin-engined plane thuds on to the tarmac, the brakes go on, the propellers go into reverse and it somehow stops.

Captain Martina, a relaxed Curaçaoan, explains as we walk the few steps to the terminal, 'You pick a point on the runway and aim for it. On Saba you don't get a second chance.'

Before 1963 when the little strip was opened there, access was very difficult indeed and visitors were few. The only landing places were Fort Bay, where there was a track up the cliff to the village of The Bottom, or Ladder Bay from which every piece of incoming freight had to be manhandled up 500 steps.

Though the richer Sabans had long had horses, the first donkey had come in 1923, much to the rage of the porters who thought their livelihood was threatened. The first motor vehicle, a jeep, arrived in 1947. Before that the very distinguished or the very infirm were borne round the island on rudimentary sedan chairs manned by four porters.

'It's a donkey on wheels,' the astonished Sabans cried as they saw the jeep.

Electricity crept up on the island in 1963. A little company provided power for six hours from six o'clock in the evening; Sabans had to wait till 1970 before they got a 24-hour power supply.

A tiny jetty was built at Fort Bay only in 1972.

Difficult access kept the few inhabitants safe. The island changed hands less often than some of its neighbours. The natural defences needed little strengthening, the islanders contenting themselves with piling up rocks on platforms at the top of steep gullies above the landing points and when necessary pulling away the supports with a rope, crushing any invader under an avalanche of stone.

Père Labat, who visited the island in 1701, recounts that in

1688 during a war between Holland and France a French corsair, Monsieur Pinel, captured a vessel which was taking supplies to Saba. The pirates seized their chance. Keeping their own ship out of sight they filled the captured vessel with their men, sailed in unchallenged to the beach where the Sabans were expecting it at nightfall, and landed without resistance. The main pirate vessel, however which should have waited for a signal from land showed itself too soon and the Sabans rumbled the plot. The stones were unloosed and the pirates forced to flee with their casualties. Rather too regretfully for a friar, one may think, he adds, 'It is certain they would have captured a lot of booty.'

It was a preposterous little place growing a little indigo and cotton but making a speciality of producing good shoes. Even the governor made shoes, says Labat, who was delighted with the six pairs he bought.

Perhaps it is the very challenge that nature poses to humans who want to live on Saba that makes the Sabans more alive and energetic than the average Statian. But whatever the reason, Saba is hospitable and much more friendly than Statia.

I went to Cranston's Antique Inn at The Bottom, the seat of government in Saba. The former government guest house, it is set in a small garden bursting with coconut palms, orange and grapefruit trees, banana plants and enormous ferns, mahogany trees and trees producing cashew nuts.

Clifford Cranston, a grave and courteous black man, and his kindly wife Matilda greeted me and showed me to a lovely bedroom. I had a view of Mount Scenery through windows framed with pink curtains and an enormous four-poster bed draped in the same material. There was no key for the door because keys were not needed at Cranston's Antique Inn.

'It'll be forty dollars,' Cranston said, adding quickly, 'but you will come to the wedding tonight, won't you? It's at six.'

'I haven't been invited,' I replied.

'I'm inviting you,' he said.

Thus I found myself swirled up into Saban society. At the end of the nuptial mass a couple of cars turned up at the church door and drove the bride and bridegroom and the principal guests sedately off along the cobbled street to the reception at the youth centre forty yards away behind the Inn.

The reception began formally enough. The bride and bridegroom sat in a row flanked by their families. As the bridegroom's godfather, Cranston was there looking particularly smart in a pink jacket. After signing the book and greeting the couple, the guests took their places facing each other on rows of seats down each side of the small hall. In the corner covered in red ribbons sat the cake. It was an Eiffel Tower of a cake, the main structure built up tier upon tier and linked to outworks of cake by little plastic gangways on which stood miniature couples in wedding dresses and tail coats, some black, the majority white, smiling out their greetings to the company. Underneath the lowest tier of the cake sat a little red plastic fountain, its tiny pump gaily sending little jets of water an inch into the air.

I expressed my wonderment at the cake to the harbour master.

'We're very good at cakes here on Saba,' he said quietly.

There were speeches, an old man sang a song, none too tunefully, the drink flowed in unbreakable plastic champagne glasses, an inexhaustible tide of canapés were borne out of the hands of the sweating helpers in the tiny kitchen by a team of young boys and girls and the dancing began to a small group of Saban musicians.

'My friends in Ungland say zey know no one who speaks such bad Unglish so ropidly.' Father Janssen, who had given an impression of severity during his sermon, turned out to be a genial missionary, self-deprecating about his command of languages. He had spent years of his life preaching in the Cameroons and was suitably scathing about the bureaucratic ineptitudes of the Vatican in the tropics. Senator Will Johnson, Saba's representative in the Dutch Antilles parliament in Curaçao, was there. Indeed from the press of people in the hall it was clear that most people in Saba were there, whites mixing with blacks with every appearance of colour blindness.

By this time a very ancient black lady in a large cartwheel hat had recovered her youth and was waltzing with every young man she could lay her thin hands on. I crept away content to my pink four-poster and went to sleep to the din of the crickets and the tree frogs.

In the morning, along I walked in the heat over to Windwardside to have a longer talk with the Senator. The road which was carved out of the side of a volcano as recently as 1960 gives sweeping views out over the ocean and every driver who passed

Ecrivain curieux des païs et des mœurs,
Il orne ses Ecrits des graces de son stile ;
Corrige en amusant, l'homme de ses erreurs,
Et s'ait mêler par tout l'Agréable et l'utile.

PÈRE JEAN-BAPTISTE LABAT *(BIBLIOTHÈQUE NATIONALE, PARIS)*

Above PORTUGUESE FORT, WHYDAH

Right PLANTATION HOUSE, JAMAICA

Below THE SLAVE COAST, AURÉLIO SILVA BORDADAGUA AT WHYDAH, BENIN

Above OLD HAVANA

Left CASTILLO LA FUERZA, HAVANA

Below LABOUR DAY, BASSE TERRE, ST KITTS

Above LE SNACK, MARIE GALANTE

Left GRANDE TERRE, GUADELOUPE

Below ESSEQUIBO, GUYANA

Above PHILIPSBURG, SINT MAARTEN

Below BAUXITE MINE, GUYANA

and every person I met called a greeting or waved. Windward-side, unlike The Bottom, is set 1,800 feet above sea level with sweeping views over the ocean and it is the place most favoured by the white population of the island. It is the seat of the local branch of Barclays Bank, housed in a building not much larger than two telephone boxes. With its tiny, well kept houses Wind-wardside was perhaps a mite too clean, too sweet, too pretty, like one of those villages in the Cotswolds or North Yorkshire where the effort to win the Tidy Village competition seems to reduce the place to a state of immobility.

As I arrived to meet Johnson a gaggle of retired expatriates, from the United States, old, frail but game, were sitting on the wide veranda of Scout's Place, a local hotel, having coffee with him. They were welcoming and interested in a stranger from London.

'Isn't that Margaret Thatcher sumptin!' said one old man.

'Yes,' I said.

They took for granted we would share an admiration of the British prime minister and a loyalty to the *Economist* magazine and it would have been complicated for me to explain to them my grave reservations about both.

Johnson is the leader of WIPM, the Windward Islands People's Movement usually referred to as 'Whip 'em'. Politics in the Dutch Windwards of Saba, Statia and Saint-Martin – which are confusingly situated among islands which the British call the Leewards – consist most of the time of two activities. The first and most important is cursing the bigger Dutch Antilles to the south, particularly Curaçao, the seat of the federal government, and the second is reminding one's electorate how when one's local opponents were in power they used taxpayers' funds to get a public road surfaced to their front door. More recently there have been the more urgent worries of what to do about the pre-valence of drugs and AIDS.

For twenty years Johnson has written, typed and published Saba's only newspaper, the *Saba Herald*. While he represents Saba in the federal government, he is no longer a member of the island's own council. Consequently the *Herald* is full of strong criticism of the fecklessness and inefficiency of that body. John-son gave me a few back copies. Lest I thought that Sabans had seriously fallen out with one another he murmured slightly apologetically, 'I lay it on a bit.'

But it will not be long before the old, isolated, self-sufficient society in which middle-aged Sabans like Johnson grew up is swept away. I strolled down from The Bottom to Fort Bay. Tucked beside the pier a big and noisy electric generator now provides all the electricity the island wants, and more. The Dutch are carving through a hill and building a new jetty which will allow cars and lorries to be poured on to an island which has only recently come to terms with the internal combustion engine. It cannot be long before hotel guests on Saba will have to be given keys to their rooms.

> 'Hell, no
> We won't go . . .
>
> 'Hell, no
> We won't go . . .'

The rhythmic couplet, once shouted in anger across the United States during the Vietnam War, came jokily over the harbour of St John's, the capital of Antigua, in the tropical sunset. Moored in the middle of the harbour, the *Jolly Roger*, her sails limp, the skull and crossbones dangling from the top of her main mast, her motor switched off, had had a good day. Five hours previously, the little wooden vessel set sail from the quayside with a full complement of cruise passengers from the *SS Starward* in whose gigantic shadow she now lay.

The *Jolly Roger*'s formula was a simple one. Passengers swapped the amenities of their enormous electronic liner on which they had sailed from Miami for the chance to pretend they were pirates and to get drunk. The *Jolly Roger* sailed cautiously round the harbour and poked her prow gingerly out into the Caribbean Sea for a league or two. Meanwhile the Bluebeards from the Bronx and the Henry Morgans from Merthyr Tydfil were fed as much rum as they could take. Usually more. It was often a job to get them into the launch to take them back to their cruise ship.

The black Salvation Army lady in white sat at the entrance to the quay with a collecting box, catching both the crowd from the *Jolly Roger* and the gamblers returning on board from the casino round the corner. A barrel-bellied T-shirt announcing 'Proud to be Irish' staggered up and dropped her a coin before struggling up the gangway back on to the *Starward*.

'It's a good spot here,' she said patiently. 'Except when it rains.'

In the brief and beautiful Caribbean twilight the harbour of St John's looked an unlikely place, with its cheery drunks, for a political scandal. But everything that happens in Antigua, innocent or criminal, happens in the harbour of St John's, the straggly capital of Antigua and Barbuda. Antigua and Barbuda is the home of the Birds, a family of politicians who have dominated the little country since well before independence and whose actions neatly illustrate the thesis that Caribbean politics are full of rascals. Rascals, I repeat, and not monsters.

The best known members of the Bird family are: Prime Minister Vere Cornwall Bird; Deputy Prime Minister Lester Bird, his second son; and Vere Bird Junior, the eldest, a senior minister who fell into disgrace.

The innocent cruise visitors come ashore there, stopping at the air-conditioned boutiques of Heritage Quay – built with Bird government help – to buy their quota of internationally standardized tourist amulets from Gucci and Fendi. (Deputy Prime Minister Lester Bird set up his office over the Gucci shop.) The innocent airborne tourists who arrive at VC Bird International Airport and who stay at the hotels built on Antigua's 365 beaches are bussed into St John's for a look at the harbour. Innocent schooners and coasters sail into the harbour from neighbouring islands with cargoes of onions or cement for the tourist trade that VC Bird founded, fostered and encouraged and on which the country continues to depend for its prosperity.

The harbour has at the same time been a scene of crime. In 1979 and 1980 it saw the trans-shipment of arms to South Africa by Space Research. This was a shadowy company whose factory straddled the US-Canadian border, which had the backing of Western governments and which was welcomed into Antigua by the Bird government. Space Research's boss Gerald Bull was assassinated by Israelis in Brussels in 1990 while working on the 'supergun' for Saddam Hussein – not long before the Supergun scandal broke out in Britain. Given the long-standing and active West Indian hatred of apartheid, Prime Minister Bird nearly lost his job because of his connection with Space Research.

But it is the criminal events of 24 April 1989 which took place in St John's harbour which cast the longest shadow over the international standing of Antigua and Barbuda and brought to a miserable climax the political career of Prime Minister Bird, trade union stalwart, fighter against colonialism, *pater patriae*. Indeed it spread gloom over the whole House of Bird.

The Birds for a long time *were* Antigua. In the 1940s VC Bird, physically a giant of a man, was the most forceful union leader in Antigua who roused the black workers against the absentee land-lords of the sugar plantations. In 1951 he led a year-long strike against the sugar owners which marked the ascendancy of unions over the bosses. He went on to found the Antigua Labour Party which has governed the country for more than three decades. He acquired the status of popular idol that even the events of 1989 did not totally negate.

In 1956 VC Bird became Chief Minister. In 1967, as the country moved closer to independence, VC Bird became Premier. The sugar industry, with its connotations of slavery and long, hard days in the blinding heat was abolished. Antigua and Barbuda became a nation of waiters living off the tourists – not a sublime calling, perhaps, but better than wielding a cutlass in a bakingly hot cane field producing sugar which had to be sold for less than it cost to make. In 1981 VC Bird became Prime Minister of Antigua and Barbuda, an independent Common-wealth monarchy.

It was to be an unruly monarchy. The Barbudan part of the kingdom was constantly in revolt against the government in St John's. A flat unattractive place, seventy square miles in area and surrounded by reefs, Barbuda was for several centuries the property of the Codrington family. Legend had it that it served as a stud farm to produce huge slaves who would work the Codrington estates in other islands. In fact the yoke of the slave master was for once comparatively light and the majority of the inhabitants had the run of the island where they cultivated their own plots and made a speciality of luring ships on to the reefs and pillaging the wrecks.

When the time for independence approached, the Barbudans were unwilling to sever the connection with Britain and had to be alternately forced and cajoled into accepting that their future was henceforward to be with Antigua and the Bird family.

Another, more frivolous political situation faced the newly independent state in the form of a long-standing English literary joke. The uninhabited rock of Redonda, a precipitous and barren volcanic crag rising 1,000 feet from the sea, was sighted by Columbus in 1493 and named after Santa María la Redonda, a church in Seville. In the late nineteenth century this hitherto useless rock began to be mined for guano, a natural fertilizer. Matthew Shiell, an Irish trader established on Montserrat, claimed it on a whim as a fifedom for his newborn son Matthew Phipps Shiell.

Fifteen years later the boy was solemnly anointed King of Redonda on the rock and given the name Felipe I. He grew up in Europe to be a novelist who acquired a certain vogue. He died in obscurity in 1947 but not before he had named a number of friends to the fantastical aristocracy of Redonda.

The heir Felipe nominated was his literary executor, another minor literary figure, Terence Ian Fytton Armstrong, who wrote poetry under the name of John Gawsworth. He took the name of Juan I but never visited the rock. Unhappily for him Gawsworth's thirst for Burgundy never matched his ability to pay for it. As he went into a long alcoholic decline in London he began trading a place in the Redondan aristocracy for the next drink. In 1954 he advertised in *The Times* that his kingship was for sale for 1,000 guineas. Prince Bertil of Sweden put down a deposit of £50 but eventually at a Privy Council held in the Fitzroy Tavern Juan was persuaded by his courtiers to relent. He died in 1970 in a state of enforced sobriety in a hospital in Chichester leaving the kingship to Jon Wynne-Tyson, an author and publisher, and his literary executor. Wynne-Tyson, as King Juan II, has been a quiet monarch, a fact that probably contributed to the emergence of a number of pretenders, including, among others, King Cedric, a black Montserratian lawyer working in the housing department of the London Borough of Greenwich.

For years VC Bird was well matched in marriage with his wife Lydia. They had six children together but later became estranged. (Even after the estrangement and when she was well into her seventies, Lydia, a forceful, devout woman continued to run the family's radio station.) The prime minister's companion for more than a decade was Cutie, nicknamed 'Evita' by the sharper political tongues on Antigua. VC Bird met Cutie when, at the age of seventeen, she was seeking, unsuccessfully as it turned out, the title of Carnival Queen.

Cutie had a child on which the prime minister doted. She also became a very rich woman, owning shops and land. Without naming her, Jamaica Kincaid, the brilliant Antiguan novelist, in her book, *A Small Place*, had this to say of Cutie.

'Overlooking the drug smuggler's mansion is yet another mansion, and leading up to it is the best paved road of all in Antigua – even better than the road that was paved for the Queen's visit in 1985 (when the Queen came, all the roads that she would travel were paved anew, so that the Queen might have been left with the impression that riding in a car in Antigua was a pleasant experience). In this mansion lives a woman sophisticated people in Antigua called Evita. She is a notorious woman. She's young and beautiful and the girlfriend of somebody very high up in the government. Evita is notorious because her relationship with this high government official has made her the owner of boutiques and property and given her a say in cabinet meetings, and all sorts of other privileges such a relationship would bring a beautiful woman.'

Disaster began to overcome the Birds that April day in 1989 when a small Danish ship, the *Elsa TH*, arrived from Haifa with a container, Number 3742, full of arms and ammunition. They had been manufactured by Israel Military Industries, and ostensibly ordered by the Antigua and Barbuda Defence Force. The order was documented with papers bearing the signature of Vere Bird Junior, at the time the islands' security adviser, minister and member of parliament. The arms had originally been destined to equip a training camp which was to be set up on Antigua by Colonel Yair Klein, a retired Israeli officer, boss of Spearhead, a military training organization with close links to the Israeli military establishment. But between the time of ordering the arms and their delivery the scheme was discovered and criticized in the US Congress. New plans had to be made rapidly. An ugly new buyer was found for the arms.

Later that day the container, after the briefest of contact with the quayside, left the harbour on board another vessel, the *Seapoint*, on its way to the drug traffickers of Colombia.

Some of these arms, 198 Galil rifles, were later captured by the Colombian forces when in December 1989 they gunned down Gonzalo Rodríguez Gacha, 'El Mejicano', one of the principal leaders of the cocaine cartel in Medellín. On 9 February, 1990 the Colombian government demanded an explanation from Israel about the captured arms. On 7 March the Israelis replied that Vere C Bird Jr had participated in the deal. Colombia was justifiably quick to complain to the Bird government.

Meanwhile, late in 1989 the *Seapoint* was arrested in the Mexican port of La Paz with hundreds of millions of pounds-worth of cocaine aboard and many of the crew with which it had left Antigua.

The whole scandal caused a great row in the Antiguan cabinet. After much pressure from Lester Bird and his supporters a committee of inquiry was appointed under a distinguished British lawyer. The affair brought new bitterness to the Cain and Abel power struggle which had already been going on there between Vere Bird Jr and Lester.

From the first Vere Bird Jr had been his father's favourite son. 'In cabinet Vere called the Prime Minister "Dad". Lester always called the Old Man "Sir",' commented one of Lester's men.

Lester, on the other hand, outshone his elder brother in the academic and the sporting sphere. Lester played cricket and football for Antigua. He won a scholarship to the University of Michigan where he excelled at athletics and then went on to study law with Vere Bird Jr at Grays Inn in London. In the 1960s Vere and Lester shared lodgings at Colindale and in Golders Green, forming part of a distinguished circle of West Indian law students who included the future Prime Minister of Grenada, Maurice Bishop.

'At that time we were the best of friends,' said Lester.

Back in Antigua Lester turned quickly from law to politics and won a seat for the Antigua Labour Party. In 1976 his father named him Deputy Prime Minister. Vere Bird Jr came into politics only in 1984 when he was named by his father Minister of Public Utilities.

Sitting in his office over the Gucci shop Lester recalled, 'When my brother joined the cabinet things started to go wrong.'

Things had certainly been wrong for years but the arms dealing case brought relations between the two brothers to such a pass that cool political observers do not discount the possibility of one killing the other in the style of the Book of Genesis.

Lester's supporters accused Vere Jr of putting round the rumour that Lester, born in the US, was never Lydia's son but the offspring of one of VC's early liaisons. On the other hand they were unsparing of Vere Jr.

'Vere Jr gives the impression of being soft . . . even goofy. *But* he's the most evil man you could ever meet,' said one Lester stalwart.

The announcement of a public inquiry, during which evidence would be taken in public, was certainly a blow to Vere Bird Jr who had opposed it. But as an influential figure in the Antiguan media, he gambled on those involved in the arms trafficking clearing their name before Louis Blom-Cooper, the English lawyer. The proceedings of the inquiry were therefore televized. He lost his gamble.

The Antiguan public, long used to rumours of corruption in high places, was fascinated by the inexorable judicial procedures which revealed the inconsistencies, rule-bending and equivocation of Antiguan and Israeli politicians, businessmen, officials and military alike. Vere Jr realized too late that by publicizing the inquiry he had dug his own political grave.

As the solemn inquiry came to its climax in a meeting hall in St John's, Blom-Cooper became a national hero, spontaneously applauded as he daily took his seat.

In his report Blom-Cooper said Vere Jr was 'unsuitable to hold public office' and that others implicated in the scandal should be replaced forthwith. Even the aspirations of Lester to follow his father into the prime ministership have been affected by the feeling on Antigua that it is time for the Bird family's political ascendancy to be ended.

In his old age VC became a tragic figure, his family at odds with itself, eldest son disgraced, what international prestige Antigua and Barbuda ever enjoyed now diminished, his own political legacy tarnished. The only consolation of his declining years was his Cutie.

Chapter Four

Guadeloupe

'Et, c'est assez, pour le poète, d'être la mauvaise conscience de son temps.'

Saint-John Persse, speech at the Nobel Prize ceremony, 1960.

At eight o'clock at night Place de la Victoire certainly is France. It could be the centre of any small, quiet town south of Nîmes. At the pavement cafe of the Hotel Normandie a slim, black Edith Piaf in a tight blouse of shocking pink and even tighter jeans is in charge, eagle-eyed and professional. The waitress's purse strapped to her belly emphasizes her slimness. Helping her is a young northern European, his blond hair held in a pony tail with a rubber band.

'*Monsieur désire . . . ?*' says Edith Piaf.

I ask for a kir and the *menu à 69 francs – crudités, spaghetti au choix, fromage ou dessert.*

Under the Stella Artois umbrellas the paper tablecloth on the white plastic table advertises Pastis, Ballantine's, Belgian beer from the Abbey of Leffe and '*Comtesse du Barry, le petit cellier des Antilles – fois gras, confits, galantines, pâtes fins cuisinés*'.

The wine list in this modest establishment would make the smart hotels in the English-speaking Caribbean blush.

Six of the tables are occupied by whites, four by blacks and one by a group of mixed races. The atmosphere is relaxed in a little local rendezvous where the regulars are at home, the bearded, bespectacled, black intellectual with his pretty Afro-haired girlfriend; young whites, tatooed and in vests, the hired crews, perhaps, of yachts in the marina. At one table a middle-aged couple chat animatedly in Dutch about *kouseband*. What, I

99

wonder to myself, is *kouseband*?

The *crudités* are fresh and crisp. Then Edith Piaf brings the spaghetti which is a delight, an enormous heap of pasta on one side of the plate, the tomato sauce with herbs carefully poured at the other – no great culinary surprise but a dish which gives evidence of having been prepared with dignity and attention. The *pichet* of Bordeaux gives no sign to my inexpert palate of having been grown anywhere but on the banks of the Gironde. A strong little coffee rounds off a totally satisfactory meal and I feel fresh energy to scribble away in the shadows.

In the warm night there is a slight smell of faulty drains. There are no beggars.

Mediterranean-looking trees grow round the ugly illuminated bandstand and on the other side of the square, its neon sign defective, a cinema stutters out its name 'RE AISSANCE'. Renaults and Citroëns slide quietly by.

A wall still carries an fading old poster

Allez Chirac
Allez la France

Lost at the end of the Place, the Darse, the waterfront which is frenzied during the day as the ferries leave for The Saints and Marie Galante, is quiet now and the waterside market is deserted.

In the morning it is different. The Place has another, less French face. Before dawn the black women of the market are loading their stalls from vans, from the boots of surprisingly smart cars or from carts. Not just the tomatoes and onions you would find in Lille or Clermont-Ferrand but a more exotic harvest. Anthurium flowers, waxy and strong, lined up in cellophane and plastic bows, bundles of cinnamon and piles of nutmeg, rows of freshly gathered pineapple.

The vast piece of plastic sheeting is covering the damaged roof of the *sous-prefecture*. It is another reminder that we are not in Nîmes. This is a hurricane zone and Hugo has just swept through the island, its immense power ripping apart and uprooting trees with the greatest of ease.

By seven-thirty the sun is already warm and the Darse is teeming with loafers, idlers, spectators, messengers' vans, parcels, taxis, mobile snack bars, lottery sellers and passengers buying their tickets for the offshore islands from the *guichets*. By eight o'clock the last passenger has gone up the gangway and the ferries, smart modern Swedish catamarans with names like *Jet-Kat* – years ahead of the struggling broken-down ferries of Guyana – are casting off on their first trips to islands. As the catamarans hum off, the Darse is almost filled with the bulk of a Cunard cruise liner whose high sides and black and red funnel will dominate the town for the day as its US passengers prepare to be whisked off for some excursion or to wander a trifle nervously round the markets and the Lebanese jewellery shops of Pointe-à-Pitre.

But unlike smaller islands Guadeloupe has too much of its own life to worry unduly about a few hundred foreign trippers. On the narrow crowded pavements of rue Frébault and rue Schoelcher, rue Lamartine and rue de l'Abbé Grégoire the bulk of the customers are locals. Those shopping, whether it be for the fine locally wrought jewellery, gold earrings, gold bangles, gold brooches and gold chains to set off their black skin, or for *brioches* and *tartelettes*, are not foreigners but Guadeloupeans. The supermarkets are full of French citizens, black and white, not tourists.

In the hubbub of the town centre there is one refuge. In a quiet, sunny little square a block away from the Place de la Victoire, church and state face each other. The Palais de Justice looks across to the Basilica of Saints Peter and Paul. Every appearance suggests that this is the white man's church. The pillared façade, indistinguishable from that of a church in a thousand other French towns bears the inelegant statues of six obvious Aryans, the two patrons and the four evangelists, manufactured by a factory in Nantes. The six likenesses are held on to the façade by steel rods as though the clergy were fearful that the black population was going to prise them off and hurl them down.

Inside, the impression that the universal church has a particularly special place for the whites is emphasized further. The plaster statues of St Teresa of Lisieux and St Anthony of Padua are white; even the archangel Michael killing a purple dragon is white. In a garish plaster copy of Michelangelo's *Pietà* a pure white Christ lies in the lap of a pure white Mary.

The basilica is a triumph of nineteenth-century white tech-
nology, being a prefabricated iron structure shipped out in bits
from France and put together on the spot, iron acanthus leaves
bolted to the top of iron columns, delicate iron lilies and their
iron stems joined together to make a pretty set of railings for the
clerestory. Patrick Leigh Fermor called it 'a boiler for a vast religious tramp steamer'.

I might have agreed with him. But it happened that my visit to
Saints Peter and Paul coincided with organ practice. High in the
choir loft the organist in his flowered tropical shirt was trying out
a Bach toccata for Sunday mass. He swayed and bent over the
keyboards, his feet bringing to life the bass harmonies. In the
warmth of the morning he brought out of the instrument noble
music such as I had seldom heard in a church. It transcended the
ugly white statues and the crude stained glass and the slightly
pastiche and artificial feeling of the prefabricated church with its
tabernacle in imported white marble. His efforts were made no
less and all the more ravishing by the fact that he chose to play
the most intricate passages over several times. I stood in the aisle
gazing up at the sublimity issuing from the powerful black arms
of the man in the tropical shirt.

Meanwhile on the altar black nuns in white veils fussed and
fretted over the red anthuriums and the white chrysanthemums
they were arranging for mass.

Some worshippers halted on their way out beside the notice
board which held the names of the winners of the tombola. The
first prize won by 'Galas, Lea' was a return ticket from Pointe-à-
Pitre to Caracas for one. How could Lea, whatever her age, be
encouraged by the Church to go to the Venezuelan capital, that
city of temptation, on her own? I wondered. Further down the
list 'Lanchet, Gilles' had to make do with a more modest, more
mysterious but much safer award, '1 objet décoratif'.

The basilica is not the only prefabricated architectural wonder
of Pointe-à-Pitre. The town produced a Nobel Prize winner for
literature, the strange white poet Marie-René Auguste Alexis
Saint-Léger Léger who wrote under the name of Saint-John
Persse.

Five blocks away from Saints Peter and Paul stands a sad,
pretty museum, whose cast-iron frame was shipped over from a
French factory a hundred years ago to serve as some rich man's

townhouse. A museum to Persse now, it seems more a reproach to, than a commemoration of the bard of cosmic grandeur, to the man of great culture and refinement who wrote of the elemental forces of nature, the clouds, the rain, the sea and above all the wind.

Saint-John Persse was a professional diplomat, a traveller, an orientalist, an anti-Vichy patriot. During his time as a diplomat he seemed to have chosen the honourable side, supporting the socialist leader Léon Blum, opposing appeasement of Hitler and suffering for it under Pétain. He refused the post of ambassador in Washington and in the Gironde jumped aboard a ship heading for Britain. The Gestapo ransacked his house in Paris and seized a bunch of his newly completed poems. The Vichy regime stripped him of his job, his goods, his Légion d'Honneur and his nationality. A generous United States welcomed him in 1940, gave him a job in the Library of Congress, a wife and the stability which allowed him to produce the poetry which would win him the Nobel Prize in 1960.

But he chose never to return to his native island in his mature years.

'That'll be ten francs,' said the attendant crossly. 'Haven't you got any change?'

The three airy floors of museum space made bigger by the great shutters opening out on to the narrow street were full of sepia photographs of the great man, keeping up diplomatic appearances in Peking or journeying in the Gobi Desert. Inscrutable pictograms, we were told, were the first Chinese translations of his poems. Here was exotica to satisfy the yearning for the exotic in the minds of the exotic people of Guadeloupe. For a European who was relishing the challenge of getting to grips with Guadeloupean society such objects were, insofar as they had any intrinsic interest, distracting. On the attic floor, however, I found a a comfortable little reading room. There I disinterred and polished up what few memories I had of Saint-John Persse from my university days, gazing at the photograph of an alert, balding, moustachioed man in a waistcoat and a spotted bow tie.

He was born a few hundred metres from where I sat, across the harbour on the Ile à Feuilles, an islet that his family owned in the Grand Cul-de-Sac Marin, the sheet of water outside the

Darse. Why had he never wanted to return?

Back to the Place de la Victoire for coffee. The square was not idly named nor was it always as peaceful as it is now. The Victoire it commemorates is a reminder of the century of bloody and pitiless rivalry between England and France for control of the riches of the Caribbean, another indication that the Antilles were in the eighteenth century as much a centre of great-power strategic rivalry as ever Berlin was in the twentieth.

The English first indicated their interest in capturing Guadeloupe in 1666. They seized The Saints as a preliminary to going for the main island but were put to flight by a cyclone. In 1703 they made another attempt. On this occasion they had to face not just the French military forces but the rage of that extraordinary French Dominican, Jean-Baptiste Labat. This larger than life friar combined the qualities of missionary, explorer, administrator, seaman, warrior, builder of fortifications, scientist, botanist and gossip.

If Labat liked anything better than a good fight against the English it was to embroider the story of it in print at a later date. Here he is at the age of fifty manning the gun of one of the defensive towers as the English under Codrington try and land near Basse-Terre,

'I went up with three of our negroes and one of our servants and I began to make our gun work. A ship of 70 guns came in front of me, but either because there were few on board or because he wanted to save his munitions he never fired all his guns and never sent me more than three cannon shots at one time; we were so close that we spoke to one another; he though once he had dismounted me and one of his men called out in French to me, White father, did they hit? I aimed my piece and scored a hit in the starboard magazine, where there was a to-do; I shouted in my turn, Was that one any good? Yes, yes, they said, we're going to pay you for it. In fact they let off three volleys so well aimed that they went through the two or three feet above our heads and we felt the wind of them very close; I served him another nine or ten times after which I went down to talk to the Governor . . .

It is certain that the thing least to fear on this occasion is the ship's cannon; it makes a lot of noise and little damage. The vessel which was in front of the tower fired more than one hundred shots, within speaking distance, without ever penetrating.

In 1759 the English had better success and captured the island. Four years later they sailed away again since under the Treaty of Paris, Guadeloupe was given back to France.

On 12 April 1782 Admiral Rodney scored one of the greatest British sea victories ever, taking on and crippling de Grasse within sight of Guadeloupe at the Battle of the Saints, tilting the balance of power in the West Indies towards Britain for two centuries. The battle, as described by Admiral Ekins a few years later, threw up one of those stories of English *sang-froid* which so delight both French and English.

'It is related of Lord Rodney by one who was a party on the occasion, that in the middle of the battle, being very thirsty, he directed one of his little attendants to mix him some lemonade. The boy, observing a lime and a knife black from former use upon a table in the after cabin, immediately proceeded to comply, and having made it, but being without a spoon, stirred it with his knife. "Child," said Lord Romney, "that may do very well for a midshipman's berth but not for an admiral; drink it yourself and go and call my steward to me."'

Nine years later the strategic battle between the two monarchies of Britain and France became something much more serious, a battle between ideologies. The revolutionaries with their unheard-of demands for liberty, equality and fraternity – which were to ripen into a brief period of emancipation – had to be stopped by those, notably the British, who did not want to see their world turned upside down.

In 1794 the British and their French royalist allies of the planter class seized Guadeloupe, for the second time in the century. But not for long. The Convention ruling in Paris had sent two commissioners to govern the island in the name of the Revolution and to put into effect the decree of 16 *Pluviose*, Year II (4

February 1794) which freed the slaves. The more forceful of the two was Victor Hugues and he was a very forceful man indeed. Hugues was from Marseilles and was by trade a barber. Some said he had made a handsome living running a brothel in Saint-Domingue.

'His character,' said a man who knew him well, 'is an unfathomable mixture of good and evil: he is bold and an excessive liar, cruel and sensitive, an inconsistent and indiscreet politician, foolhardy and pusillanimous, a despot and a flatterer, ambitious and villainous, often loyal and direct . . . ambition, avarice, the thirst for power determine his virtues, direct his desires and come together in his soul: he loves only gold, sells gold, works for and by gold . . .'

Arriving off the coasts of Guadeloupe on 6 May 1794 with a motley collection of 1,470 soldiers in a ramshackle flotilla to bring Revolution to the French West Indies, Hugues and his fellow commissioner, Pierre Chrétien, were aghast to see the island, which they thought was in French hands, under the command of the English.

They landed with difficulty and published a stirring address,

'To all the citizens of Pointe-à-Pitre and other adjacent townships.

'Citizens,
   For two months the English have made of you without distinction a people of slaves: the arms of the Republic have come to break your chains, to deliver you from your captivity and halt the persecutions under which you had been for long destined to be the unhappy victims. But now that you enjoy the full range of a liberty which you pledged yesterday, through the hands of your national representatives, to defend with the last drop of your blood; now that you must prepare to honour your oaths, the commissioners appointed by the National Convention invite you to sign up at the town hall as paid national volunteers; for the formation of several battalions which they decree shall be organized; they further decree that the authorities of the town shall immediately open a register to this effect and that the recruitment shall be carried out among citizens of all colours.

'At Pointe-à-Pitre, 20 *Prairial*, Year II of the one and indivisible French Republic.

'Signed: Pierre Chrétien and Victor Hugues.'

The force brought together by this appeal contained some of the first former slaves to enlist freely under the republican flag. They proved more determined than the English veterans and their French monarchist allies under General Graham.

On 7 June 1794 the English were swept from the town by the revolutionaries in a battle fought in the square. The winner was Victor Hugues. His shadow was to lie heavily over the square, over the island and over the West Indies for years.

Hugues was quick to carve his name on Guadeloupe. As soon as the town was recaptured he decreed in language which Stalin or Kim Il-Sung would have understood,

'There shall be formed within twenty-four hours in the commune of Port-de-la Liberté (hitherto Pointe-à-Pitre) a military commission to judge all those accused of offences against the liberty of the people, the security of the republican government, the unity and individuality of the Republic, of all thefts against the Republic and tending to its detriment by wastage; in a word of all crimes against the national interest.'

In a typically self-assertive report to the Convention in Paris he wrote *à propos* the royalists,

'We are at last masters again of the colony and the ground is no longer sullied by the satellites of the tyranny. 650 immigrants have been guillotined or shot for having joined forces with the English.'

The blood from the severed heads and the headless corpses, they say, turned the water in the Darse red.

'You don't want to see them. They're marginal to society here,' said the friendly and efficient Guy-Claude at the tourist office, keen on his job of promoting Guadeloupe as a cosmopolitan holiday resort. 'Why not go to Marie Galante . . . ?'

'They're dying out anyway,' added his colleague.

Both remarks whetted my appetite to visit the Blancs-Matignon, the lost white tribe of Guadeloupe.

'*C'est un très petit groupe. La consanguinité, tu sais . . .*,' said François, the black reporter at France-Antilles. 'Get in touch with Madame Louis-Carabin at Moule. She's the mayor. She knows all about them. They live at the Grands Fonds at Moule.'

The bus for Moule leaves from the proletarian end of Pointe-à-Pitre. A half asphalted piece of waste ground behind the ugly modern post office is the *gare routière*. No less French than the Place de la Victoire, its Frenchness is that of the Paris suburbs with a higher population of immigrants. It is the ante-chamber to that France that the poorer emigrant from Guadeloupe will get to known. For these were proper solid French semi-slums, ugly but well built. Not the sort of cardboard and corrugated iron shacks that you found people inhabiting on the English-speaking islands.

Tall blocks of flats, their entrances protected by fierce metal grills, their walls daubed and sprayed with political slogans, made a grim amphitheatre to the bus station. Passengers were catered to by a decrepit Citroën van selling hot dogs.

'*Viv UPLG*', said the walls.

The separatists of the *Union pour la Libération de la Guadeloupe* – or rather of 'Gwadloup', the spelling preferred by the creole-speaking separatists – either had strong support from the flat-dwellers or had a group of very dedicated slogan painters.

From fourteen floors black women gawped out with their young families from sparsely furnished apartments. Teenagers and the young black unemployed loitered by the small buses.

'C'est pour Moule, monsieur?' I asked.

'C'est pour Moule, monsieur. Montez.'

The bus was nearly empty, just one passenger beside myself, a ten-year-old girl going home from school and concentrating hard on her ice cream. Half a dozen passengers wandered in in the next ten minutes. But it was not until the driver, a sharp 25-year-old black, got in that it was borne in on everyone that bus-driving in Guadeloupe was a commercial enterprise demanding marketing skills of a high order and a deftness with human bodies similar to those shown by the men who are employed to pack Japanese people into underground trains.

Hilaire wove his vehicle to the front of the column of buses departing for various parts of the island. With the eye of a hawk he tooted the horn at every potential passenger on the pavement, urging every new customer into the bus and placing each newly arrived on the folding seats which could be erected in the gangway. When each row of four seats contained at least five people, when there were three giggling Indian girls standing at the front and when the authorized capacity was comfortably – or in our case uncomfortably – exceeded did we set off. As the only white in the bus I felt no hostility. A white in his fifties was clearly a rarity but not necessarily an unwelcome rarity. Five hundred metres from the bus station Hilaire stopped the bus and an older driver took over. Presumably he returned to the bus station there to exercise once again his ability to pack forty people into a space designed for twenty-seven.

In a moment we were bowling along through the scruffy villages of Grande Terre – Abymes, Vieux-Bourg, Morne à l'Eau, which no Parisian tourist is ever taken to, dusty agglomerations half-buried in the ripening sugar cane, each with its Mairie, its Postes and its First World War monument. Every few hundred yards we would stop to take on a new passenger or to let one off. The alighting passengers tendered an exact fare or received change from the unchallenged computer memory of the infallible driver. Those who got out of the rear door of the bus came up to offer their coins to the driver who tossed them on to a red cloth by the gear lever at his right hand.

At every stop there was a quiet '*Avancez. Asseyez-vous, s'il vous plaît.*' Better individual productivity was never found on a Ford production line; better civic discipline was never shown in ancient Thebes.

Within an hour we were at Moule, an untidy suburban place which had long ago lost out in importance to Pointe-à-Pitre. Its shark-infested waves rolling in from the Atlantic do little to attract the tourists from the calmer Caribbean waters of the other side of Grande Terre.

The town has regularly taken the brunt of any hurricane hitting the coasts of Guadeloupe and the main square of the town still showed grievous signs of the passage of Hugo. Sheets of gleaming new corrugated iron had replaced the old which had been ripped off and scattered like so much silver paper over the already untidy countryside.

Breakfast time was five hours away and a distant memory. Was there likely to be any place capable of curing hunger pains in this out of the way *bourgade*? Beside the Hôtel de Ville in the main square was the awning of a Délifrance shop. Within stood a friendly black waitress who single-handedly managed the spotless snack bar which would have warmed the hearts of the directors in Paris of France's fast gourmet chain. Unsuccessfully she tempted me to a sandwich of *thon mayonnaise*. I opted for a crusty *baguette* filled with ham and a glass of beer which I followed with a slice of Royal Poire and a strong *café crème*. Restoration was rapid and complete and I returned to the size I measured before I had been squeezed into the bus.

Within another thirty minutes I had found Madame Louis-Carabin, a handsome middle-aged woman of powerful managerial talents who had been born to be some town's mayor. She summoned a municipal Mercedes and an East Indian chauffeur and sent me on my way to Grands Fonds to visit Madame Roux, a Blanche-Matignon who was on her mayoral staff. How many municipalities in the rest of the Caribbean would have on hand a Mercedes and a chauffeur to ease the life of some casual visitor?

We bowled back on the Route Nationale along which I had just come and turned off southwards towards Les Grands Fonds and the house of Madame Roux. At one point there was a signpost to Château Gaillard and I wondered what romantic settler had chosen to name a village on Guadeloupe after the medieval fortress in the River Seine which I had clambered over with my friends from school in my early teens. After a few miles the flat fields of cane gave way to small hills and gullies and suddenly the skin colour changed.

'*C'est un Blanc-Matignon*,' said the chauffeur, satisfied that he had carried out the mission of carrying me to the promised land which had been entrusted to him by Madame.

A handsome white boy of ten with reddish hair, very proud of his new bike, was standing chatting to some other equally handsome white boys on the outskirts of a hamlet. This was Matignon.

After a few stops for directions we found the house of Madame Roux, a woman in her early thirties of pure white complexion who stood with her equally white mother-in-law awkwardly on the verandah of a solid brick-built house. No tumble-down ruined slum, as I had been led to expect, but a respectable dwelling which would not have been out of place in 10,000 other French villages.

'He's a journalist. Madame Louis-Carabin sent him,' said the chauffeur.

The tiny white colony of the Blancs-Matignon is something of a mystery – or if not a mystery an occasion of controversy and embarrassment on Guadeloupe. Some five or six hundred of them live in the hilly interior of Grande Terre conserving up until recent years the pure white colour of their skin and rejecting all sexual involvement with the black or with the East Indians, like the chauffeur, who are to be found on Grande Terre. Were they the ruined progeny of aristocratic families sent out to the colonies in the centuries when France was a monarchy? Did they have some distant connection with the Princes of Monaco? Were they the remnants of the refugees from Hugues, revolutionary terror and his guillotine? Were they the irreducible kernel of resistance to the law of 1848 which emancipated the slaves? Was the ignorance and embarrassment of other Guadaloupeans towards them the result of a feeling that they were a degenerate and in-bred community whose sexual practices sullied the island? Was their rejection of miscegenation doubly embarrassing in a *département* of France where blacks, whites and browns all shared a technically equal citizenship but where the blacks in reality were by most reckonings at the bottom of the pile?

If there were answers to these questions I quickly realized they would not be forthcoming from the Mesdames Roux.

No, they did not know anything about the old stories. The only people who knew about things like that were the old men and, *vous savez*, the old men were dead. Why did you not go to see the Ramade family at Sources?

We went back to the car and drove on for a mile or two along the twisting hilly road until we came to Ramade's supermarket, an old-fashioned grocery store with the family quarters above.

'He's a journalist. Madame Louis-Carabin sent him,' said the chauffeur a second time.

Honoré Ramade emerged from the interior of his neatly kept

shop. In a cautiously friendly manner he and his teenage son Francis, both as white as the Roux, invited me to sit down on the first-floor veranda of their house, a well-built affair befitting a prosperous country shopkeeper.

'I've come,' I said, 'because I'd heard many stories of your community and wanted to get to know it and its history.'

'Yes,' they replied guardedly.

I pulled out the island's best guide book and showed them apologetically the less than flattering references to their inbreeding and their indigence, references which bore little relation to the lower middle class comfort I had seen that day in the Grands Fonds.

Sensing a sympathetic listener Francis, more eager and more coherent than his shopkeeper father, started telling the Blancs-Matignon story, quietly at first but then with the increasing passion of a young man with a sense of pain, injustice and frustration.

'We are not backward. Look, you can see. We've got the roofs back on our houses after the hurricane quicker than anyone. Have the rest of them got their roofs back on? Have they? Do we look like idiots here?

'We're misunderstood. All we want is to be left in peace. We're less than a thousand. Less than eight hundred. Say five hundred or six hundred. We keep ourselves to ourselves. That's all.

'Take that guide book of yours. It says we live in huts. Do you call this a hut? Look at the joinery on that ceiling. My father did all that joinery since the hurricane. How many people could do joinery like that? How many of the other people' – he gestured with his head towards the universe of black Guadaloupeans outside – 'could do joinery like that?

'That guide book calls us "Romade". The name is "Ramade". Can't they even get the names right?'

As the hour ticked by and with the urgent pride and romanticism of a young man, Francis talked about the past.

'We had vast lands you know. They were taken off us. Today we haven't got a fraction of what we had in the past. We had lands. We had vast plantations. And castles. In Brittany. And other places. I personally don't like the name Blancs-Matignon. I prefer the name "nobles". We were nobles, you know. Some years ago we wrote to Prince, Prince . . . '

'Rainier?' I offered.

'Yes, that's it, Prince Rainier, to see if he could find out more about our roots. We never got a reply. Perhaps it went to the wrong address.'

The final crushing argument was left to last. Pointing to the gleaming German-built saloon parked in front of the shop. '*Et not' p'tit BM' là-bas!*'

Congenital idiocy was not a circumstance which allowed a family to buy a BMW. We paused.

'But was a community as tiny as this, specially one which was beginning to intermarry,' I asked, 'not running the risk of disappearance?'

Francis thought. 'Perhaps,' he said softly. 'Perhaps.'

'Why,' said Kathy, the black tour guide, 'is the cock the symbol of France?'

'We don't know,' shouted the jolly party of French tourists in the bus on Marie Galante.

'Well, the cock is the only bird which manages a song when it's got both feet in the shit.'

'Ha, ha, ha,' roared the trippers, warmed by their mid-morning visit to the little rural rum distillery. 'He, he, he.'

We headed back to Grand Bourg, the chief town of the flat little island twenty-eight kilometres from the mainland. We passed through a little village with a metal statue of a soldier standing as its memorial to the First World War.

'When you see a French *poilu* on a war memorial in a place like this,' said the widow from Clermont-Ferrand, 'it makes you think.'

After a while she added, 'I still think we ought to give these blacks their independence . . . '

Marie Galante was the quintessence of the sugar economy. The crop first came to this flat little island in 1650 and by the first half of the nineteenth century there were 106 sugar factories on an island of 158 square kilometres and a population of no more than 10,000. The riches financed the building of the habitations, the great houses, of which one remains, the Château Murat. It stands, abandoned now, a few kilometres outside Grand Bourg on a slope overlooking the sea. Its grey classical stone façade is approached by a stone staircase and is made splendid with four stone pilasters and five bays of windows, a solid memorial to a dynasty of sugar planters in the early nineteenth century.

The high life, which 200 hectares of land worked by slaves afford the Murats within their château, was summed up in the inventory taken in 1839:

'A large mirror 76 inches high by 45 inches broad in a gilded frame, valued at 250 francs,

'A gilded copper lamp holding 30 candles, valued at 400 francs,

'Fourteen bed sheets in fine cloth nearly new valued at 10 francs each,

'Eighteen sets of cutlery, two soup spoons, four large spoons for stew, two sugar spoons and eighteen gilt spoons, valued at 1,300 francs.'

The windmill with its six sails was valued at 30,000 francs, the boiler house where the sugar was boiled at 40,000 francs, the land 157,450 francs. The inventory listed 175 male and 132 female slaves. The value of the slaves was put at 290,568 francs. Each of these human beings was therefore worth rather less than the Murats' cutlery.

But the rich world of sugar fortunes was soon eclipsed. All began to fall apart soon after the nineteenth-century heyday of the sugar barons. The difficulties of the Murats and others started five years before the taking of the inventory. In 1834 the British abolished slavery in their empire and any black who could cross the difficult water from Marie Galante to the British island of Dominica on the southern horizon could escape serfdom and become a maroon.

Six slaves – Pierre, 40, Auguste, 39, Jean called Malocaye, Etienne, 30, Montlouis called Piloti, 28, and Petit Maxime, 54 – had escaped to Dominica. No one knew where 16-year-old Saint Jean had gone.

The estate could stand the loss of half a dozen slaves, but the decree of 27 April 1848 abolishing slavery for the second time and for good on French territory spelled ruin. The loss of slaves assisted by maladministration meant that the property which in 1839 was worth 668,161 francs and 46 centimes was seized in 1868 and sold to pay off family debts for no more than 103,950 francs.

Dominica, the British island which separates Guadeloupe from Martinique, was again to be a refuge for Guadeloupeans seeking freedom a century after emancipation.

On the plane I met a black from Marie Galante who had fled to Dominica during the *dissidence*. Comfortably retired now after a life living in exile in France working in a garage, he had as a teenager sought to serve the best interests of his country by fleeing his island.

At the beginning of the Second World War the French Antilles and Guyane declared for Vichy. Admiral Georges Robert was Pétain's high commissioner in the region, installed in Martinique. He had at his disposal a small fleet including the cruisers, *Esterel, Quercy* and *Barfleur*, a flotilla of submarines, the aircraft carrier *Béarn* and the cruiser *Emile Bertin*, the most precious of all which, after escaping arrest by the Canadians in Halifax, had brought the Banque de France's stock of 300 tons of gold to the Caribbean.

Robert assigned the cruiser *Jeanne d'Arc* to anchor in Pointe-à-Pitre to ensure Guadeloupe's attachment to Vichy under the administration of Governor Constant Sorin; and the bishop of Guadeloupe, Monsiegneur Genoud, accepted the honorary post of chaplain to the cruiser. The Place de la Victoire was renamed Place du Maréchal Pétain.

In November 1940 Robert ordered the famous letter of Madame de Pompadour to the Duc de Mirepoix, the French ambassador in London in 1753 to be broadcast on Radio Guadeloupe. In every detail, down to the name of the British sovereign, it expressed the point of view of Vichy and the centuries-old Anglo-French mistrust:

'Your letters, *Monsieur le Duc*, always please me . . . The English know neither how to eat, live or work with taste. I am sincerely sorry you are obliged to live in the land of roast beef and insolence. I doubt you are any more exposed than we to the evil reasonings of these proud island dwellers. It seems they want war; their perplexity is to find an honest pretext. But the real and biggest crime of which France is guilty in their eyes is that of re-establishing its navy. The step taken by the parliament of England in naturalizing

Jews has astonished all Europe; the old Marshal says that the religion, laws and customs of the Israelites render them incapable of being good citizens and good subjects; they are always a people apart who form a state in a state and to whom one should not extend privileges but with discretion. One supposes that gold, like love, makes all men equal. France has known for a long time that the precious metal is all-powerful in England and that everything there is on sale; peace, war, justice and virtue. You are happy with the politeness of the King George's ministers; we are not with their policies. They suffer from a great failing in negotiations; that is that they always want to mislead. Take care that you are not and think always of your fatherland and your friends.'

Words from history, however true they might have rung, did not convince everyone in wartime Guadeloupe, particularly when the British and US naval blockade brought about severe shortages on the island. With no way to import wheat, bread had to be made of cassava. The breadfruit trees were never more highly prized. Bananas never failed. What little salt there was on the island was eagerly sought after, some companies awarding their employees salt bonuses if they were good timekeepers. Alcohol distilled from sugar cane was mixed with what oil there was to make 'Antillean petrol'.

Against the pro-Vichy rule of Robert and Sorin there rose the *dissidence* and brave spirits, disgusted with pro-Nazi rule in Guadeloupe, defied the naval patrols round the island to get away to Dominica.

'It was years ago but I remember it to this day,' said the man from Marie Galante about his time in the *dissidence*. 'My friends had persuaded a fisherman to take us from Marie Galante to Dominica. There were about twelve of them and I just went with them. It was all very secret and I didn't tell my parents, I just jumped into the boat at midnight. We didn't get over to Dominica till it was dawn and it was very, very rough.

'We landed at Marigot on the Atlantic side of Dominica. It was right across the island from the town of Roseau. There was no road so we had to go round the island in a boat again. We got to Roseau and they gave us rations. I had no shoes and I can remember the warmth of the asphalt on the streets on my feet.

'I was too young to join the Free French army but some of my friends did. Some never came back.'

In 1943 with the tide of war going against the Germans, de Gaulle's Free French sent their representative to Guadeloupe and Robert slunk away later to be arrested when he re-entered liberated France.

In the rue Schoelcher two formidable bookshops face each other, the Librairie Générale and the Librairie Antillaise, guardians of Caribbean France's pride in the intellect. No bookshops in the English-speaking Caribbean can rival the intellectual wealth in which these two shops trade. Thrillers, poetry, history, economics, the latest Parisian novels, philosophy, cookery, *Le Monde*, guidebooks, the local communist newspaper, postcards, are crammed into the bulging shelves which fill the busy shop which is always full of customers. The cash tills are never idle as the Guadaloupeans feed their brains on the rich fare.

The day I was at the Librairie Générale was a special day. Maître Felix Rodes, distinguished lawyer, grand old man of the Guadaloupean left and supporter of autonomy for the island, was signing copies of his latest work on the first abolition of slavery. A man of mixed race, sure of himself, a touch imperious even, he wrote his careful dedicatory phrase in the copies of his book that the queue of reverent readers presented at his desk – after, that is, he had prudently checked that they had a receipt from the till.

I did not buy his volume on slavery. Keener on trying to judge the strength of modern day links between Metropolitan France and its former colony, I bought his *Liberté pour la Guadeloupe; 169 jours de prison*, an account of his imprisonment in 1967 for his part in demonstrations against the de Gaulle government.

I offered him the book, the receipt and my card. In a strong, neat hand he wrote,

'To Hugh O'Shaughnessy of *The Observer* who will through this book relive the massacres of 26, 27, 28 May 1967 perpetrated under de Gaulle by the French colonists which produced 87 dead, 300 wounded and 500 imprisoned. This book is the testimony of the defence lawyer jailed and sent to the French State Security Court because he defended the Rights of Man and Liberty.

Pointe-à-Pitre 3 February 1990,

Felix Rodes.'

The first few pages of the book set out robustly enough the Guadeloupean case for independence.

'Guadeloupe is that strange little island in Central America where for three hundred years two sets of men have played cat and mouse: the White being the cat and the Black the mouse. The East Indians who arrived on the island at the end of the last century are looked on a little like the *anolis*, those little insect-eating lizards much enjoyed by tom cats . . . '

He went on to develop the theme that little had changed since emancipation, that slavery had been merely replaced by assimilation, assimilation of a population which felt itself to be a nation and which wanted to be free to administer its affairs itself. In a conscious tribute to the British form of decolonization he pointed to the fact that Guadeloupe was surrounded by a group of former British colonies which were either independent or at least self-governing.

Behind the façade of a *département* of France, supported by large infusions of government cash from Paris, enjoying a higher standard of living than most of the rest of the Caribbean, there was clearly still a degree of envy in Guadeloupe for the more modest but independent regimes of Barbados, or St Lucia or St Kitts. I walked out into the crowds in the rue Schoelcher with the Guadeloupean dilemma of affluence versus independence buzzing round in my head.

Chapter Five

Grenada

'We shan' allow imperial-isim to triumph,'

Grenadian soldier, October 1983

I pick my words carefully when I say there is no more beautiful island in the Caribbean than Grenada. Some perhaps can equal it, none can surpass it. In this Eden Nature has been wildly prodigal with gifts: Man for his part has done nothing to spoil and what little he can to embellish. Life may not be easy in Grenada and for many it may be less than fulfilling but it is lived in among finest surroundings, in different spots tranquil, pleasant, languid, rugged and fertile.

A tiny place little more than twenty miles long and ten miles wide it seems, with its mountainous variety and twisting roads, much, much bigger. The island rises from perfect sandy beaches, sheltered bays and rugged coasts through tiers and tiers of forested hills dripping with waterfalls to dank mountains and high, cold moorland. Every evening the sun goes down into the broad sea to the west, a dramatic red ball which leaves the warm velvety glow of night.

On this stretch of land plants luxuriate, particularly spices. The possession of one nutmeg tree, the Grenadians say, means a man need do no more work to survive than beat its trunk and collect and sell the fruit which falls. And the *myristica fragrans*, the great nutmeg tree, sixty feet high, yields not one but two spices, nutmeg itself, the hard kernel which grows inside its protective shell and the aromatic mace, the filigree which grows round the nutmeg kernel between it and the shell. It is no wonder that the flag of Grenada includes a nutmeg.

119

There are clove trees, allspice and the cinnamon trees whose delicate bark can be harvested and dried to prepare that incomparable spice. Roots of ginger and the saffron-coloured turmeric are there to be dug up. There is cocoa, with the pods spouting comically from the tree trunk itself. There are coffee and bananas, coconuts, sugar cane and breadfruit, luscious grapefruit, avocados, guavas, cashew nuts, lemons, limes, sugar apples, tangerines, tamarinds to make delicious refreshing drinks, soursops and mangoes for puddings.

Flowers are in profusion all the year round, jasmin, jacaranda, bougainvillea, angel's trumpet, cup of gold, spider lily, Turk's cap and hundreds more. And there are loofahs to be picked and dried if you need something to tone up your skin in the bath.

While pale trees fringe the coast the road across the island goes through groves of bamboos and at its highest point is fringed with ferns as big as houses.

It is difficult to do justice to the luxuriance of the island in print. It is the sort of natural earthly paradise that would have enchanted Rousseau, Bernardin de Saint-Pierre and the French romantics.

While the ice age scraped and moulded Europe and all the northernmost and southernmost parts of the planet into geographical sobriety the tropics, which were never frozen to silence and immobility, were left free and warm to multiply and luxuriate. Aeons later the overwhelming result is there to be enjoyed in Grenada.

The island is ruled from St George's, a miniature Rio de Janeiro in the Caribbean, a town totally in keeping with the natural world about it and a living set from one of Verdi's more extravagant operas. Around the harbour, a pair of drowned volcanoes overlooked by the eighteenth-century Fort George on a promontory, the commercial life of the town goes on in shops, offices, warehouses and garages. The volcanoes provide geological effervescence; they may be drowned but they are not dead. On 18 November 1867 late in the afternoon the water level in the harbour dropped about five feet and in one part began to boil as sulphurous fumes began to be given off. Then the water welled up four feet above normal, tossing round the Carenage. This happened several times and a great deal of damage was done.

The citizens and the notables live in houses built on streets, some frighteningly steep, which offer increasingly panoramic views out to sea or into the hills the higher they climb.

None of the buildings is outstanding but many of the Georgian and Victorian ones, St George's Anglican Church and St Andrew's Presbyterian Kirk are very pleasant, the sort of places of worship which might have been built in any small English town around 1800. The aspect of the town has not changed much since it was described by Sir William Young, Bart, a visiting MP, in 1792.

'St George's is a handsome town, chiefly built of brick, and consists of a good many houses. It is divided by a ridge, which, running into the sea, forms on one side the Carenage, and on the other the bay. Thus there is the Bay town, where there is a handsome square and marketplace and the Carenage town, where the chief mercantile houses are situated, the ships lying landlocked and in deep water close to the wharf. On the ridge just above the road of communications between the towns, stands a large old fort.'

The Grenadian fizz has since been provided to the architecture by a bizarre gothic *palazzo* commissioned by some megalomaniac bishop. This is where the Irish Christian Brothers who run Presentation College now live.

The hills themselves are protected by Fort Matthew, Fort Adolphus and Fort Frederick. Throughout its recorded history Grenada has been an effervescent place. On his third voyage Christopher Columbus sighted it on 15 August 1498 and may or may not have landed there. It somehow got called after Granada, the city in Andalusia, a name which became corrupted to La Grenade in French and Grenada in English. It seems the English were the first to try and colonize the place in 1609 but a party of 208 colonists, harassed by the fierce native Arawak, quit after nine months. Charles I of England gave it to one of his nobles in 1627 more or less at the same time as it was theoretically included in the domains of Cardinal Richelieu's East India Company. After a false start in 1638 the French made a better job. A certain Parquet bought Grenada, St Lucia and Martinique from the company. He landed with 200 men in 1650 and gave the Caribs 'some knives and hatchets and a large quantity of glass beads, beside two bottles of brandy for the chief himself' for their rights to the island. The French incursion eventually led to the war in which the Caribs were annihilated.

The native population having been wiped out, the French experimented by bringing over criminals and undesirables from the metropolis. But that did not succeed. They then started importing Africans to work on the plantations of tobacco and indigo. By 1753 12,000 had been brought in. By the late eighteenth century the island was a vastly prosperous enterprise for the estate owners and began to be hotly contested between the British and the French. By the Treaty of Paris which ended the Seven Years' War the island went to the British. They doubled sugar production and the island became a great deal more important to Britain than New York and its major colonies in New England.

It was not long before the French, at war once again with Britain, made a stupendous military effort to regain the island. A great fleet carrying 10,000 men under Admiral d'Estaing invaded Grenada in 1779 and routed the British garrison of 540 men of whom only 90 were regular soldiers. Under the Treaty of Versailles however the island was restored to Britain.

The troubles between Britain and France were not yet over. After the execution of Louis XVI in 1793 and a new outbreak of war between the two countries, revolutionary France was happy to make mischief for her old enemy. She pledged support to the remaining French colonists in Grenada, who had been discriminated against by the returning British, if they rose up against British rule. A coloured planter, Julien Fedon, son of a French father and a slave mother, and owner of the Belvedere estate, took the commission from Victor Hugues, and the French revolutionaries on Guadeloupe rose on 2 March 1795 before eventually being put down.

The French legacy persists still in place names – Sauteurs, Grand Etang, L'Anse aux Epines, Morne Jaloux – family names – Marryshow (from Maréchaud), Julien, Belizaire – and the Catholic religion.

With emancipation in 1833, new sources of labour had to be found. Some Africans were brought in as indentured labourers, while others came from the East Indies, Malta and Madeira and the racial make-up became as mixed as anywhere in the

West Indies.

In 1843 the new owners of Belvedere changed the course of Grenada's agriculture by first planting the nutmeg which had been brought to the West Indies from the East Indies, the islands which were formerly Dutch and are now Indonesian. A year or two later a pest hit the East Indian nutmeg and Grenada became the world's principal supplier, exporting the spice whose flavour was – and still is – prized for its quality.

In the twentieth century the politics of Grenada were caught up in that same relatively gentle pressure for political emancipation and eventual independence which pervaded the rest of the Caribbean. The British rule, though hardly on the side of rapid social progress, was not so repressive as to spawn the sort of heroic and intransigent liberation movements that fought off the French in Algeria and Vietnam. There was nothing like Kenya's Mau Mau in Grenada.

Grenada produced gentler figures such as the middle-class Afro-Irishman, William Galway Donovan, who produced a newspaper with the motto 'A Naked Freeman is Nobler than a Gilded Slave', and his disciple, Theophilus Albert Marryshow, who admired the British Labour Party and wanted racial harmony on the island.

> 'For all his noble gifts,' said Gordon K Lewis, the historian of the West Indies, with characteristic acerbity, 'Marryshow, at the most, was a West Indian Fabian, a Royalist-Loyalist whose staunch Whig constitutionalism never permitted him to fight the colonial power except on its own polite terms.'

Grenada was to produce its own monster in the person of the trade union leader Eric Gairy. He was a cross-eyed, extravagant, ridiculous bully without principle, who covered his white suits with extravagant decorations from obscure governments and fancied himself as a ladies' man. But, even at his worst, he could not stand comparison with serious tyrants of the Caribbean like Fulgencio Batista in Cuba, François Duvalier in Haïti or Rafael Leonidas Trujillo in the Dominican Republic.

By the time he was twenty-nine in 1961 Gairy had moulded his own trade union, the Grenada Manual and Mental Workers

Union, into the first effective force through which workers were able to challenge the power of the employers. As in many other islands in what was then the British West Indies, political power resided in control of the trade unions. Gairy based himself on the union and on his Grenada United Labour Party which fought a running battle with Grenada National Party, the vehicle of the richer Grenadians. He ruled the island uninterruptedly from 1967 to 1979 with a mixture of charm, violence and corruption, relying on an organized gang of ruffians, the Mongoose Gang, to ensure that his will was done.

In 1973 the fusions of two new groups founded the previous year by left-wing intellectuals, the Movement for Assemblies of the People and the Joint Endeavour for Welfare, Education and Liberation (JEWEL) gave Grenada its first political party with any pretension to ideology, the New Jewel Movement. The NJM, lead by Maurice Bishop, yet another of those London-trained lawyers who emerge to lead political movements in the Caribbean, was violently opposed to Gairy.

The following year Grenada came to independence from Britain – in the dark. Strikes against Gairy rule meant there was no electricity. Gairy himself used independence and a seat in the United Nations for every sort of mischief, serious and ludicrous. On the one hand he collaborated with the Pinochet dictatorship in Chile and on the other he called for a UN investigation into flying saucers.

In 1979 in the first popular *coup d'état* against a constituted government in the English-speaking Caribbean, Gairy was overthrown by the New Jewel Movement and fled into exile. Though the NJM did nothing to change the status of the island as a monarchy or remove Queen Elizabeth as head of state it called for revolutionary change in Grenadian society. It achieved little concrete success though in the future historians may judge that it forged rather deeper foundations to Grenadian nationalism that the egregious Gairy had been able to lay.

In international affairs Bishop aligned himself rhetorically closely with Cuba and his model Fidel Castro in spite of the fact that the NJM government did little to change Grenadian society and did not have even Cuba's limited resources to devote to international affairs. Grenada under Bishop also sided with a rather bemused Soviet Union. Throughout his premiership, however, there continued below the surface of politics the fierce personal rivalry that had existed since their boyhood between him and Bernard Coard.

Late in 1983 Bishop and his followers were arrested and put to death by the followers of Bernard Coard. They were shot in the picturesque old bastion in St George's which Bishop himself had rechristened Fort Rupert in honour of his own father who had been murdered by Gairy's men. The stage was set for the US invasion and I was sent to write about it. My journey in 1983 to this Eden, which was in crisis and virtually blockaded, was an extraordinary experience.

Shortly at two o'clock in the afternoon a twelve-foot canoe powered by an outboard motor and laden with journalists sneaked its way among the yachts and schooners out of the harbour in Union Island. We had come to Union Island in a charter aircraft because all flights to Grenada itself had been suspended and because Union Island is the nearest point of foreign soil to Grenada. Union Island belongs to St Vincent and lies a short distance away from the island of Carriacou which belongs to Grenada. As we left the anchorage a blond with short legs and bare breasts waved to us from a particularly luxurious vessel which flew the French flag. It felt as if we were going into battle. We were certainly going towards battle. Once out of the harbour nature heightened the sense of combat. We were in a sea scattered with rocks and islands which looked as though it had been a battleground of giants who had left the sharp debris of their struggle lying around the horizon.

We were seven beside the boatman and his young mate. The doyen of our number, bearded and attired in a smart straw hat was Bernard Diederich, the expansive New Zealand-born correspondent of the New York weekly *Time* who had written encyclopaedic books on the dictator Trujillo in the Dominican Republic and on 'Papa Doc' Duvalier in Haïti; bespectacled, more scholarly-looking and more reserved was Don Bohning of the *Miami Herald*, the US newspaper which devoted most space to Caribbean and Latin American coverage; the *Washington Post*'s man was Ed Cody, possibly the most intellectual of our number; Morris Thomson, a tall, thin impatient man, quietly unashamed of his homosexuality, was writing for the popular US newspaper *Newsday*; Greg Chamberlain of the *Guardian* seemed to have devoted a lifetime to studying the Caribbean and was particularly knowledgeable about Haïti; Claude Urraca, French photographer of the Sygma picture agency, was in a few days' time destined to take pictures of Grenada which would be printed all over the world.

We reached the rickety pier at Hillsborough, the main village on Carriacou, about four in the afternoon and were welcomed and had our passports stamped with no difficulty. We had reached Grenadian territory, if not the main island of Grenada, and we had done so, as far as we knew, long before any of our rivals. We were in a high state of elation. We had eluded the blockade which its neighbours had imposed on Grenada and now nothing could take away from us the fact that we were on Grenadian soil at a momentous time.

Our first task completed, we now had to ensure our onward journey and we soon found another boatman, Alfred, who promised he would take us on in the morning the thirty-four nautical miles to St George's, the capital of Grenada, in his vessel the *Odin C* which, unlike our boat that afternoon, had a decking and a small cabin for shelter.

We settled into the Silver Beach Hotel, a pleasant rather run-down establishment where guests had their own bungalows. Before dinner we met Edwin Stiell, the young administrator of the island of 10,000 people, and Milton Coy, a clever but rather self-effacing young man who was the political education officer. The two took us on a tour of the hilly thirteen square miles of the island pointing out the houses of the retired people from Canada and the US who had continued living on Carriacou despite Bishop's revolution.

Carriacou is one of those many islands of the Caribbean which look better from the sea than from the land. There were few buildings of any note and neither the accidents of geography nor the vegetation held much charm. For us journalists its attraction lay in the fact that it was at the centre of a crisis and that we had been accepted by those Carriacouans whom we met with open friendliness.

Over a dinner of lobster we celebrated our arrival. Morris asked for a bottle of the famous Barbadian rum remarking, 'If I'm buying it, it better be Mount Gay.'

Naturally there was an atmosphere of crisis and uncertainty on

Carriacou, that feeling of not knowing what tomorrow would bring or what shape society would be assuming next week. It was an atmosphere I had come to know well during political crises and *coups d'état* in Latin America. Indeed the uncertainty had often been the narcotic of excitement, that feeling of riding some mustang, which came with reporting and writing on Latin American life and which, I was happy to remind myself, I would seldom have been able to enjoy had I been confined to a job in Britain or somewhere else in Western Europe. But it was more unfamiliar in the usually calmer circumstances of the politics of the Caribbean.

With Stiell and Coy we talked long into the night about Bishop's murder and the split in the revolution. I wrestled hard but thankfully, as I had done many times before, with the task of understanding the current situation of a foreign place. Though Grenada was one of the few islands in the Caribbean which I had never visited, I had once had a brief encounter with Bishop in the twilight at the independence celebrations of Belize in September 1981. Surrounded by a strong bodyguard he had struck me as arrogant, overweening and unsympathetic and somewhat condescending to our host the self-effacing Belizean Prime Minister, George Price.

At six, as dawn broke, I was woken by the radio which some kind member of the hotel staff left on the porch of my bungalow. The US troops had invaded, the announcers said. All members of the people's militia and all medical staff should go to their assigned posts.

The announcers, a man and a woman, declaimed antiphonally between snatches of martial music, 'We shall fight them on the beaches. We shall bury them in the sea.' I was one of the group who thought and said the invasion was wrong and illegal, a fact that distanced me politically from some of the US members of our party and in particular from Don Bohning to whom I must have been a sore trial. But I was once again exhilarated, not just at having reached Grenadian territory but also at having arrived in time to experience the invasion.

After a quick breakfast we went down to the harbour where Alfred and his young mate were awaiting us on the *Odin C*, and before seven-thirty we were on our way.

Under a sun which quickly became very hot the *Odin C*

chugged southwards down the western side of the smaller islands of the Grenadine chain for several hours while we listened for whatever news the radio could give us. On the eastern horizon we went past the Sisters, the inaccessible and queerly named Kick'em Jenny surging 700 feet out of the sea, Les Tantes, the Ile de Caille and the Ile de Ronde, their French names recalling the time when France battled for paramountcy with Britain in these waters.

Grenada, if the US government was to be believed, was beginning to reacquire in the 1980s the strategic importance it had enjoyed in the 1780s and had lost when the Europeans started the cultivation of their own sugar beet. As the *Odin C* ploughed on we began to pick up the explanations of the US case.

The invading force were quick to set up 'Radio 1580', a US controlled station which put the political case for the invasion and broadcast messages in English to the People's Revolutionary Army, and in Spanish to the Cubans on Grenada to surrender. 'Radio 1580' was part of the large propaganda effort that was mounted with extreme care and attention by the US government for the occasion.

The journey was as interesting from the point of view of the sea creatures as it was for the politics. Flying fish accompanied us most of the way rising up and skimming for yards over the sea. Every so often we would see the fin of a shark.

As we came abreast of the northern point of Grenada the invasion which we had been following on the radio finally became visible. Large helicopters moved across the horizon. Not long afterwards two US jet aircraft came out to have a look at our boat, followed half an hour later by two helicopters from the invading force. We believed, but could not be certain, that they would not attack us. As the *Odin C* moved southwards towards St George's the invasion became more palpable. We saw jets strafing the international airport on the far south-western point of Grenada which Cuban construction workers had been building and were now defending and ships of the force became visible in the far distance. The sound of the bigger explosions came over the water.

Radio Free Grenada, the station of the government, was soon silenced and the broadcasts from the US side, which featured messages from President Reagan became more confident, reporting that the main points of the island had fallen.

The nearer we got to St George's and the more explosions we heard, the more unhappy Alfred became at the prospect of putting into the harbour. As midday came and went we squabbled out there in the Caribbean, Alfred claiming payment before he sailed any closer, Don for our side stoutly swearing he would not get a cent till we were at the quayside. The *Odin C* traced a zigzag course as the argument swayed one way and the other.

Then came the eeriest moment of the lot as Alfred, finally prevailed upon, turned the *Odin C* into the mouth of the harbour under the rock of Fort Rupert which for two centuries had guarded the seaward approach to the Grenadian capital. The place was completely and utterly still. A rent in the green roof of one of the buildings in the fort showed that it had suffered a direct hit from the air but neither on the quay, nor in the streets nor at the windows could we make out any signs of life. St George's might have been bewitched for all we could make out. The mutter of the boat's engine seemed to echo round the bowl of the harbour. The boat nosed up to the quayside of the Carenage and no one came either to help us make fast or to challenge our arrival in Grenada.

At that precise second, however, on the very dot of time when I started to scramble on to land there was an almighty crash and scream as a US jet came in to strafe the positions of the Grenadian army in the town. The attack was immediately countered with deafening anti-aircraft fire from a Grenadian position a few hundred yards from where we had landed. I threw myself on the ground seeking whatever protection a rim of coping stones on the quay could offer.

Alfred seized his money from the hands of Don, put the *Odin C* in reverse and buzzed out of the harbour as fast as its motor would take him.

The essential fact had in the meantime been borne in on us: St George's was not in the hands of the invading forces but still under the control of the People's Revolutionary Army. We did not realize it at the time but we were even closer to death than we had thought. We later learnt that as the *Odin C* came into the harbour it was in the sights of the rocket launcher of a PRA soldier who had every reason to believe that we were some scouting party from the invasion force. He was about to fire his weapon and kill us all when a fellow soldier recognized Alfred as a Grenadian.

We had hardly recovered from our noisy introduction to St George's when four soldiers came up in a jeep to find out who we were. Our passports were checked and it seemed to be accepted that we had entered the state legally through Carriacou on the previous day. We were nevertheless told to stay in the fire station-cum-immigration office, the nearest building on the Carenage to the spot where we had landed.

We spent a very long and rather frustrating afternoon under the guard of some Grenadian soldiers, listening to the sounds of battle yet unable to see much. The combination of explosions of battle and the total silence of the cowering town was even more eerie than the complete absence of noise and movement which we had noted as we came into the harbour. At one point there was a loud explosion and some rejoicing from our Grenadian guards who reported that they had brought down a US helicopter.

Late in the afternoon the US forces managed to set light to Butler House, a former hotel sited on a promontory across the harbour mouth from Fort Rupert which had been used as the seat of government. The firemen started their East German fire engine and sped off. But to no avail and they eventually returned tired and dejected. As the sun went down the flames from the still burning building cast a red glow over the town and the once secret papers of the Grenadian revolution floated down and lay on the Carenage. I should have started collecting them. The invaders certainly did, using them to make up and publish tendentious accounts of the workings of Bishop's government which tried to make him appear as some Caribbean combination of Pol Pot and Béla Kun.

With the telephone service from the fire station cut off and we journalists confined to the premises, those in our group who worked for daily newspapers were increasingly desperate to phone through their dispatches. A hundred yards along the Carenage the lights of the offices of Cable and Wireless were burning bright and mocking us. In the early evening we were finally given permission to go and see if it was still working. It was locked and empty. There was no alternative but to batter the door in. But even when we had done so we could not make any of the telexes inside work. We returned disconsolate but then a jeep and a few soldiers appeared and we set off in search of ways to contact the outside world by telephone. The automatic telephone system within the island was working and was doubtless humming busily in the darkened houses but it was impossible to obtain a line to the outside world. We careered round the unnaturally quiet, darkened town looking for a telephone operator while one of the young soldiers, full of revolution and the ardour of battle, rained down curses on the invaders who still had not penetrated the town.

'I ready to die for me contry,' he shouted as at breakneck speed we negotiated the hairpin bends of the blackened, inert town, totally safe from the threat of any oncoming traffic, 'to lay down me life against imperial-isim. We shan' allow imperial-isim to triumph.'

The attitude of the Grenadian soldier that night reminded me of earlier fights to the death in Grenada. His words recalled the dying defiance of the Caribs to the French in the seventeenth century. Having kept the whites at bay for a century and a half the Caribs decided to make a stand against the latest European incursion. They called in reinforcements from nearby islands and the French did too. French firepower prevailed, as Spanish and Portuguese firepower had elsewhere in America, and the Caribs were now beaten. The last forty of them jumped off a cliff at the northernmost point on the island rather than be captured by the colonists. The cliff is still known as La Morne des Sauteurs, the Hill of the Leapers, outside the town of Sauteurs.

The soldier was a latter-day version of one of Julien Fedon's troops. The flag Fedon received from Hugues in Guadeloupe bore the words, 'Liberté, Egalité ou Mort'. And the fight he put up was a tough one. It took more than a year, with help provided to George III by the King of Spain, to control Fedon, who at one time commanded all but a small section of the island. Fedon was let down by his logistics. He had captured a few cannon with which to defend his camp, but he had no cannonballs and for projectiles his gunners had to make do with pieces of sugar wrapped in sacking. Logistics were soon to prove the Achilles heel of the Grenadian forces.

The comparative powerlessness of his French revolutionary allies, unable to take on the might of Britain, also let Fedon down. His redoubt at Belvedere was finally stormed by two regiments. But Fedon himself was never taken and the circumstances of his death remain a mystery. All that was ever discovered about his fate was an abandoned canoe found in the sea between Grenada and Trinidad which contained a compass known to have belonged to him. In much the same way Cuba was too weak and the Soviet Union were too far away, to help save the Grenadian revolution.

The Grenadian soldier, a corporal, reminded me, too, of more recent historical parallels. He brought to mind the lone sniper I had heard but never seen on the day of Augusto Pinochet's military putsch against the Allende government in Chile. As one or two of us journalists took refuge in the British embassy in Santiago on 11 September 1973 we heard from the roof above us the crack of a small rifle in the hands of some brave soul taking pot shots at the heavily armed troops below. The shots, which sounded as if they were coming from a light .22 rifle, ended after a helicopter identified him and silenced him with a burst of fire.

After some searching round town we found the supervisor of the telephone exchange and she consented to come and try to make it work for us. Despite her best efforts, however, she was not able to contact any number outside the island and we remained isolated from the world.

By about seven-thirty in the evening the fighting seemed to be dying down and we were finally allowed out to find beds for the night. These we found at the St James' Hotel directly across the water at the other end of the Carenage, a few yards away from the entrance to Fort Rupert where Bishop and his companions had been murdered a few days before.

The St James' turned out to be a delightful, old-fashioned place which exuded an intense, if slightly faded, respectability, reminiscent of the Pension Vauquer in Balzac's *Père Goriot*, designed for *les deux sexes et autres*; alternatively it would not have been out of place in New England. It was built mostly of wood and had a superb view of the harbour. The food, we were to discover, was such as used to be served in the more modest British boarding schools, and the bathrooms were provided with showers fitted with horribly dangerous Brazilian electric water heaters. But that Tuesday night it was nirvana.

It was presided over by the elderly, reserved but warm-hearted Miss Pearl Patterson. She exuded the concern for her guests that the big hotel chains advertise but only rarely provide.

Most of her guests who, one assumed, were not generally tourists but rather commercial travellers up from Port of Spain or down from Bridgetown, had quit Grenada. Virtually her only guests were two elderly ladies. 'I couldn't have abandoned my own mother so how could I have left Miss Fitt and Miss Bertrand?' Miss Patterson asked simply.

Like everywhere else in the town the hotel was without electricity but in the candlelight Miss Patterson and her helper, who were clearly not used to attending to the demands of foreign journalists, served us cheese, bananas and beer, as I noted at the time, with all the solicitude of a maiden aunt for her adolescent guests.

The seven of us, resigned now to the inevitability of being incommunicado for at least the next few hours, blew out the candles and settled to as much of a night's rest as the US aircraft and the Grenadian anti-aircraft fire would allow. It was reminiscent of the blitz in London in 1940. Within a few hours Grenada would be in US hands, to the joy of the vast majority of the population who saw it as a deliverance from the Leninist extremists who had killed Bishop.

Two years after the invasion I was back to see Ronald Reagan make a triumphal visit of a few hours to the island. There were two tiny demonstrations against him as he arrived on the island, the first staged by the Maurice Bishop Patriotic Front, who claimed intellectual descent from the murdered leader. It was a disaster. The half a dozen speakers scheduled to address the crowd in the market place outnumbered the crowd itself. The second was less organized but more spirited. Along the Carenage a few Rastas, harassed by the police on the eve of the president's arrival, burned the Stars and Stripes and catcalled and jeered as the presidential cavalcade swept by on its way to Queen's Park, the cricket ground and sports field on the northern edge of town.

The US leader was greeted there with great enthusiasm in mid-afternoon by tens of thousands of Grenadians. Watching at the scene I was reminded of the days of the invasion when we journalists had ventured out from the St James' Hotel to Queen's Park to see the commander of the invading US Marines.

Meanwhile Lieutenant Colonel Ray Smith lounged in his armoured command post among the throng of troops and armoured vehicles which were squeezing in on the flat piece of ground beside the sea. As we waited I fell into conversation with a marine signaller who, noticing my English accent, starting reminiscing about his times in London. It turned out that he had gone to the same London school I had. His father, Chuck, who had known Ronald Reagan when he was governor of California, had been posted to the security staff of the US embassy in Grosvenor Square.

The colonel received us in an affable way, reclining in his armoured command vehicle like some oriental pasha. (It was only later we learnt that the rivalries and lack of coordination among the various US units had made the invasion a groping logistical and tactical nightmare.) He presumed, since the majority of our group worked for US publications, that we were all disposed to help him in his task of subduing the island. Though I thought little would be gained by expressing to him or to my US colleagues my unwillingness to do anything that might be construed as cooperation in an operation I considered illegal, I constantly reminded myself that I should not extend the bounds of good manners into a willingness to assist in solving the US tactical problems.

Bernie Diederich, Claude Urraca and I had gone to Queen's Park twice to talk to Colonel Smith while the US troops were waiting to take over St George's. Tanteen Field is an open space near the centre of St George's whose name, adapted from the French word *tontine*, a form of communal land ownership, is another reminder of the island's French past. There on the second day of the invasion someone had dumped the corpse of the pilot of one of the US helicopters which had been shot down on the previous day, the remains of which lay a few yards away in a patch of burnt grass. The picture Claude took of the dead man, spread-eagled on the ground, was one of the most affecting images of death and suffering taken during the war and went some way to counter the fallacious impression that the government in Washington was trying to give of the invasion being some painless military picnic.

On our second visit we told Colonel Smith of the body and he promptly sent a detachment of marines into town to recover it.

Within a few days too the wreckage of the helicopter, a memento to the skill or luck of some anonymous Grenadian fighter, was also carted off.

When President Reagan went past Tanteen in 1985 the grass had grown again and there was nothing to indicate that a dead pilot had lain there. Grenada's link with the United States seemed almost stronger than the link with Britain had been in the old days. Conservative values and business ethics had taken the place of the revolutionary fizz of the New Jewel era. Those who had supported Maurice Bishop were lying low; those who had supported Bernard Coard were lying very low indeed.

As the years passed, however, the invasion, which loomed so large at the time, seems less and less important. The large allotment of financial aide that the Grenadians hoped would be granted to them by the United States government has not materialised, nor has there been much private investment. Sir Paul Scoon, the governor-general who was appointed in the time of Gairy and who was retained by the revolutionaries, continued at his post when the US forces came and after they left. Gairy himself survived to fight elections. In Grenada motorists continued to drive on the left, schoolchildren to sit British examinations, cricketers to play cricket and Grenadians to be ruled over notionally by a Queen of Grenada who lived far away in a place called Buckingham Palace.

Chapter Six

Utopia?

'If there were but a snug secretaryship vacant there – and these things in Demerara are very snug – how I would invoke the goddess of patronage; how I would nibble round the officials of the Colonial Office; how I would stir up my friends' friends to write little notes to their friends! For Demerara is the Elysium of the tropics – the West Indian happy valley of Rasselas – the one true and actual Utopia of the Caribbean Seas – Transatlantic Eden.'

Anthony Trollope, *The West Indies and the Spanish Main*, 1860.

The very old black man peering through the decrepit spectacles sat in the sun on the wall beside the brown river in the corner of Stabroek market, that cast iron turretted cathedral of commerce in the centre of Georgetown. Behind and above him were the bows of a little coaster, beached on the mud, battered and abandoned, plants and flowers growing out of her wheelhouse. In the river the high-sided ferry was making her way crabwise over to the western bank three-quarters of a mile away, her prow pushed upstream into the river, defying the mighty Demerara to wash her out into the Atlantic.

I was in no hurry.

'Good morning,' I said to the very old black man.

'Good morning, my lard,' he replied brightly.

'Are you well?' I asked, hoping to conceal my confusion at being the object of such a form of address.

'Yes, I am, tank the Lard.'

A pause.

'De blessins of Jesus Chris' fall upon you and give you healt' and happiness an' blessins and bounties,' said the very old black man taking my white hands in his.

Confidence having been established between us there was no stopping him.

'May Jesus Christ protect and guide you, my lard.'

He told me his name was Mr Cox and how he had salvation inside him. He recounted how he had come over from Barbados when he was very young and how he had obtained jobs, including one sailing up the rivers on the hulk which rose up behind him. Now, he said pointing to a friendly and alert looking East Indian with a vegetable stall bursting with yams and other roots, he was being looked after by his friend.

'He his,' the very old black man said with immense dignity and grace, 'he his purveyor of ground provisions.'

But there was one subject on which he was dying to unburden himself.

'Dere is no finer race on eart' dan de white people. Dey are de Chosen of the Lard in de Bible, in de Ole Testament. Dere is no finer people.'

I demurred wordlessly and uncomfortably but, if he noticed, he did not care.

'Mr Burnham rob de kin', nice white people of dere gold and dere diamons an' trew dem outa dis contry. Dat was a wicked, wicked ting to do an' I hope that de Lard gib us light to welcome de dear, sweet, white people back to dis lan'. What Mr Burnham do was wrong, my lard, my father, my brother. It is time for de good white people be back in dis lan'.'

I made noncommittal noises and tried to change the subject. Pursued by the blessings of the very old black man I eventually left. I felt privileged to have won his confidence, happy to have been the repository of his trust. Mr Cox, and many Guyanese thereafter, bore out what Trollope said of them in when that country was the colony of British Guiana or BG,

'I never met a pleasanter set of people than I found here, or ever passed my hours much more joyously.'

But I was disturbed at the import of his message.

Georgetown is a city of graciousness and folly, of assurance and precariousness, of righteousness and violence, of ugliness and poetry.

There is no street in Georgetown to rival Paramaribo's beautiful Waterkant but Main Street, the principal avenue of the city, is a strong contender. Parallel rows of trees shade the broad pedestrian walk which is provided with comfortable benches in the middle of the straight avenue. A carriageway at each side takes the traffic. The avenue is lined with the best houses in Guyana, solid, gracious, white-painted wooden structures – the Anglican bishop's palace, the former governor's residence and others – Victorian but vaguely reminiscent of the Dutch style and recalling the century or more when the colony was Dutch.

In the commercial centre of the city the architecture becomes more fantastical. The City Hall was built in 1887 to the design of a Jesuit missionary but could equally have been erected by Mad King Ludwig of Bavaria. It is an exercise in South American gothic folly with slim turrets, pointed roofs and medieval ornamentation, the entrance protected by stout wooden doors which might have come from a Welsh castle. The whole thing could be removed brick and tile to the kitsch surroundings of some Disney world where people would pay money to gawp at it as the home of Snow White and her Seven Dwarfs.

Georgetown claims, like Paramaribo, and doubtless many other cities, to have the largest wooden structures in the world. St George's Anglican Cathedral was built five years after the City Hall and soars 143 feet into the air, its architects creating with hardwood what the medieval masons did with stone in York, Canterbury, Ripon and Salisbury. But the texture is different from any English cathedral. There is no holy gloom. The midday sun comes streaming in through the windows, and doors are flung open as if the building were gasping for air in the heat. Inside, rescued from an earlier structure, are the memorials to the colony's worthies.

From 1813 comes this elegant obituary in stone:

Sacred
to the memory of
Captain William Peale
the brave and highly respected commander
of His Majesty's Brig *Peacock*

whose death was glorious as his
life was honorable.
Engaged in unequal combat with the
American ship of war *Hornet*
a cannon shot in mercy terminated his existence
almost at the same moment that his
gallant vessel consign'd to the deep
gave a worthy sepulcre to the remains of
her lamented chief.

The Catholics have their cathedral, the Church of Scotland has a pretty but mouldering little church, there are halls for the black followers of sects with names like the Unified Four-Square Gospel Church of the Cherubim while bungalows crowned incongruously with bulbous domes in what looks like papier-mâché or with stuck-on oriental window frames cater for the Muslims and Hindus from among the East Indian majority.

Much of the rest of the centre of town, though laid out along airy avenues broad enough to carry a drainage culvert, is a conglomeration of untidy shops and offices, alleys and markets, all drained by the system of dykes and culverts laid out by the clever Dutch. Beside the river lies Tiger Bay, a few blocks of poor housing where the choke and rob gangs, the whores, the pimps and the fences sit safe from outside interference.

The most important structure in Georgetown is not a building. It is the sea wall behind which the city crouches at high tide lest the brown Atlantic sweep it away. The great dyke which stretches for miles cuts off all view of the sea. It gives airy Georgetown, which, unlike Pointe-à-Pitre, was never a snug well defended town, a strange feeling of introspection, a feeling of being cut off from the rest of the world. Parts of the city bear the names of former sugar plantations such as La Penitence or La Bonne Intention. On the very edge of the city the cane fields start, demonstrating that there is more money in growing sugar in the rich alluvium than in devoting space to meandering suburbs. As the cane grows it shuts off the city from the south and the east in the same way as the sea wall shuts it off from the north and the Demerara shuts if off from the west. The cane fields surround Georgetown with an impenetrable mass of green cut through at right angles by water courses. These water courses serve as drainage and as thoroughfare for the barges bearing the cut cane and give the countryside a strange look, half tropical, half Dutch.

> 'To the rear,' wrote Trollope, 'there is an eternity of sugar capability in mud running back to unknown mountains, the wildernesses of Brazil, the river Negro, and the tributaries of the Amazon – an eternity of sugar capability, to which England's colony can lay claim if only she could manage so much as the surveying of it. "Sugar!" said an enterprising Demerara planter to me. "Are you talking of sugar? Give me my heart's desire in Coolies, and I will make you a million of hogsheads of sugar without stirring from the colony."'

The supply of labour has always been at the centre of politics in a country which is the size of England and Scotland and whose population is no greater than that of a large English town. But Trollope's enterprising Demerara planter doubtless did achieve his heart's desire. Labourers were brought in by the shipload from India in the last century to take the place of the emancipated slaves who were no longer obliged to work in the cane fields. They were accompanied by smaller drafts of Chinese, 13,500 in all, a sad group of which only 2,000 were women. Though the Chinese population shrank to around 2,000 many eventually made good. One of them was Arthur Chung, the first President of Guyana from 1970 to 1980.

The Portuguese, too, came, mainly from Madeira. The supercilious British colonial masters treated them very much as second-class Europeans. They were excluded from the census returns of 'whites' and were – and indeed still are – referred to dismissively as 'Potogees'. But they were astute enough to move rapidly out of the cane fields. By the 1840s they were moving into trade and eventually became, with the East Indians, BG's shopkeeper class. They were particularly good at running rum shops.

The Portuguese were a well-knit community which maintained culture, language and traditions into the twentieth century. In July 1898 they celebrated the 400th anniversary of Vasco da Gama's discovery of the route to India. The *Daily Chronicle* of 16 July reported,

'The day was given up by a large majority of the Portuguese to festivities. Nearly all their houses or business premises were decorated with flags or bunting, and in some cases, such as the Ice House, the Kingston Chocolate Factory (Both belonging to Messrs D'Aguiar Bros) the houses of Mr Jorge Camacho, Vice-Consul for Portugal, and Mr Abreu, of the firm of Messrs Rodrigues and Abreu, the decorations were tastefully arranged and elaborate. During the day nearly all the rum-shops, which bore signs of the national rejoicing, were closed. The Concert in the Gardens was most enjoyable and the selections rendered were well chosen, as will be seen from the programmes appended. The Consul for Portugal, Mr D'Almeida, arrived about 3:15 o'clock, and he was received with the Portuguese National Anthem (*Hymna da Carta*) played by the Militia Band.'

But while the Portuguese built up their trading enterprises and the Amerindians, the first inhabitants of the country, mainly stayed on their rivers and in their forests and were seldom indeed seen in Georgetown, the economic sheet anchor of the colony remained the plantation where the majority of the East Indians stayed. Sugar was sown on the flat, rich, black lands in an extensive geographical area unrivalled by any of Jamaica, Barbados or the 'little islands' of the Eastern Caribbean. The sugar industry, too, was the focus of racial tension between the two most important communities, the blacks and the East Indians.

There has been enmity between blacks and East Indians for generations. After emancipation the blacks felt they could bargain with the sugar owners for the price of their labour. The arrival of the East Indians weakened the blacks' bargaining position – as it was meant to do. The blacks fled the land which had been the reason for their enslavement and moved into the towns. Those who had the will and the ability eventually graduated to jobs where they could wear a collar and tie. The East Indians from the moment they arrived embraced the land, seizing the opportunity of buying little plots or 'gardens' once their indentures were served out.

The blacks had been ripped from the womb of their different African cultures in the most inhumane way and dumped higgledly-piggledy on a foreign shore, many of them physical orphans, all of them cultural orphans. For their part many of the East Indians, far from being loaded forcibly on to slave ships, had volunteered to serve indentures. Between 1835 and 1917 238,960 arrived. They adopted British Guiana as a land of opportunity and, whether they were Muslims or Hindus they brought over their well-codified religions and their strong cultures with them from the sub-continent.

As far as the employers were concerned everything was to be gained by setting one race against the other and there was no advantage in promoting racial harmony. Whether assiduously spread by the employers or merely welling up from mutual incomprehensions and antipathies, racial stereotypes emerged and took deep root in each culture. The blacks were caricatured by the East Indians as feckless, idle, flashy bullies totally lacking culture. The blacks caricatured the East Indians as physically weak, scheming, money grubbers, always plotting to take advantage of the easy-going good nature of their African neighbours.

The East Indians, or 'Indo-Guyanese', so multiplied that today they are the largest and wealthiest community in Guyana. Whether they have stayed in agriculture or gone into business, the East Indians, hard-working, frugal and oriented towards their families, have grown richer than the more happy-go-lucky blacks. The census results, kept secret after they were computed, are said to show that five out of every ten Guyanese are now East Indians while about four of every ten are blacks. But the Blacks, or 'Afro-Guyanese', have been unwilling to cede control of a country built by the sweat of their enslaved forefathers to what might be regarded as a set of Johnny Come Latelys. After all the size and importance of the East Indian community went against the pattern established in all other parts of the British West Indies – except Trinidad – where black majorities quietly and peacefully took over the political hegemony that had been exercised by the British before they retreated from the empire after the Second World War.

A black lawyer set out to make sure that, when the British quit, power would be left in black hands. Linden Forbes Sampson Burnham, the second son of the headmaster of the Methodist Primary School, was born in 1923 in the village of Kitty near Georgetown. His brains won him a university scholarship to

Britain. His silver tongue won him prizes for oratory and the
presidency of the West Indies Students' Union in London.
When he was twenty-five he was called to the Bar at Gray's Inn.

In his book *The Middle Passage* V S Naipaul, the Trinida-
dian-born writer who finds so little good to say about the peoples
of the West Indies, had this to say about him in 1962.

> 'Mr Burnham is the finest public speaker I have heard. He
> speaks slowly, precisely, incisively; he makes few gestures;
> his head is thrust forward in convinced, confiding, simple
> but never condescending exposition; he is utterly calm, and
> his fine voice is so nicely modulated that the listener never
> tires or ceases to listen.'

For three decades until his death in 1985 Burnham fought a political duel with the leader of the East Indians. By fair means and
foul Burnham always won.

Cheddi Bharratt Jagan was born in 1918, one of eleven children of a Hindu sugar estate foreman and his wife. He was an intelligent, hard-working boy who scraped a university education
in Washington and Chicago and returned to Georgetown with a
degree in dentistry. He also returned with a wife, Janet, the
daughter of Jewish immigrants to the United States. She became
the nurse at his dental practice and his companion in Marxism-
Leninism.

In their early political days in the 1950s Burnham and Jagan
set up the People's Progressive Party. But before long Burnham
set up his own People's National Congress taking blacks with
him, and Jagan stayed with the People's Progressive Party.
Though both parties attracted clever men and women of all
races, the most talented of whom Jagan and Burnham appointed
to their cabinets, the PPP membership became predominantly
East Indian while the PNC was overwhelmingly black. This was
an irony since the entrepreneurial East Indians who followed
Jagan because of his race had little in common with his ideology,
while the anti-Communist East Indians who joined the PNC
were often reviled by other members of their race.

Jagan made no secret of his Marxism-Leninism, but the
United States was determined to prevent that ideology estab-
lishing itself in any part of America. Jagan fell into Washington's

disfavour while Burnham and his PNC were looked on approvingly by the US and its British ally in the 1960s, as British Guiana approached independence. When the PPP won elections and formed a government in the last days of colonial rule there was panic in Washington. The US government called for measures to be taken against him, a call which was more or less reluctantly heeded in London. Taking advantage of Premier Jagan's mistakes and an outbreak of communal violence, British forces landed. The voting system was changed and Burnham, seen as a bulwark against Soviet wiles in the Western hemisphere, came to power. He took British Guiana into independence in 1967 as Guyana, a monarchy with Elizabeth II as its queen. In 1970 the kingdom of Guyana became the Cooperative Republic of Guyana and the PNC was declared to be 'paramount'.

In his first years in power Burnham hewed to a conservative pro-Western line. He supported the US in Vietnam, refused to condemn Ian Smith in Rhodesia, cut ties with Cuba and generally adopted unyielding anti-Communism. But later a more self-confident Burnham, conscious that the West would never move against him for fear of allowing Russia in, took a delight in provoking the imperialists, assuming positions in the Non-Aligned Movement, nationalizing the big foreign investments in sugar, bauxite and banking and taking money from the Soviet bloc and China where he could.

As sugar prospered, so had the fortunes of the biggest British company, Bookers, which by the time of independence owned by far the largest acreage of cane and had developed retail stores, import agencies and a thousand and one other businesses. BG, it was said, did not stand for British Guiana but Bookers Guiana. Burnham took over Bookers. Burnham also nationalized Reynolds and Alcan, the US and Canadian companies which dug out and exported bauxite from mines in the interior.

Time and again Burnham rigged the elections in favour of the PNC. The favourite method was to stuff the ballot boxes. The government collected them in from the outlying polling stations to a central counting centre but forbade opposition representatives, who had the right to oversee the voting, to accompany them. During the journey to the central counting centre votes for opposition candidates were changed for votes for PNC candidates. In some elections an overseas voters roll was prepared which was liberally sprinkled with imaginary voters. The overseas voters, real and imaginary, cast a healthy majority of their ballots for the PNC.

But no word of disapproval was spoken by Western governments. No displeasure was voiced in Moscow or Peking either, for the hierarchs there did not want to be seen to be contradicting an 'anti-imperialist' leader of the Third World who proclaimed he was 'marching towards socialism. When Burnham died, his ideological mantle as president was taken on by his successor in the presidency, Desmond Hoyte.

Guyanese were left prostrate and bewildered by the choice between the electoral fraud and gerrymandered black racialism of the PNC and the Marxist-Leninist façade cobbled on to the PPP, the party of the East Indians.

Many times in this big and immeasurably fertile country, sparsley inhabited by little more than 500,000 people, I was to hear the message of Mr Cox. All but the government supporters complained that black government had failed, comprehensively failed, and that the country was seizing up.

That there would be trouble for me in Guyana was clear as I presented my passport to the immigration officer at the international airport in 1990. The flight from Barbados had been different from most in the Caribbean. There were no obvious tourists on board. Guyanese conditions being what they are and despite the natural wonders of the country, Guyana does not attract many tourists. No one goes to Guyana casually. The little plane was as full of interesting people as any steam packet nosing her way to Georgetown a century before. A very old and frail white man was eased on to the seat in front of me by a lady who could have been his daughter.

From the seat behind I overheard a conversation about them.

'I don't know much about her except that she regularly rides to hounds in Ireland,' said a voice.

In another seat sat Father Petry, an English Jesuit returning to the mission field. There were a few blacks displaying Rasta colours.

Beside me sat Tom Aitken, a friendly eager man with a family timber business in Scotland near Loch Lomond, an *Observer* reader who had spotted me with the paper in the departure

lounge in Barbados. He was going to buy a boatload of indes-
tructable greenheart in Guyana which would be sold to make piling and groynes for sea defences. As it turned out, I was lucky to
meet him. We passed the flight chatting over glasses of rum.

At the immigration control, however, I was on my own. In
Burnham's time the Guyanese government had shown it had not
liked what I wrote about Guyanese domestic policies. In August
1972 I had written a survey of Guyana in the *Financial Times*,
one of those regular editorial exercises which aimed to be in-
formative without being too controversial. I had mentioned the
racial tensions and added,

> 'It was plain that Mr Burnham stayed in power as the result
> of widespread irregularity in the overseas postal vote and
> the proxy vote. The same system will be in operation in the
> forthcoming elections, which are expected to take place
> from one month to another. Mr Burnham's position is
> backed up by the fact that both the police and the army are
> predominantly African descent.'

I knew the government had a long memory and that in any case
procedures had not changed in eighteen years. The last time I
had been in Georgetown was in 1978 when I had been sent to report on the Jonestown massacre. This was the tragedy in which a
deranged religious fanatic from California called Jim Jones who
had been adopted and protected by Burnham had persuaded his
followers to poison their children and then commit suicide by
drinking the same poison themselves. My reports – every journalist's reports – were intensely embarrassing to the regime even
though we were prevented 'for health reasons' from going to
Jonestown itself.

The woman police constable looked at my visa and asked me
suspiciously what I wanted to do in Guyana.

'I am a journalist,' I answered.

'But what you goin' to do?'

'I am a journalist,' I repeated.

'Yes, but what you goin' to be doin'?'

'I am a journalist,' I repeated again unhelpfully.

'I'll have to see de sergeant.'

The sergeant, after further scrutiny of my visa, finally decided to allow me into the Cooperative Republic.

Things were much worse than I had remembered them twelve years earlier. Constant power cuts in the city made daily life difficult and industrial production impossible. In order to alleviate the situation a set of generators which would help the venerable machines which had been producing electricity for decades was found and bought in the United States. The scheme failed when the barge which was carrying it reached Georgetown and amid public indignation and suspicion of corruption an official enquiry had to be held. Those who had the money bought stand-by generators which zoomed into action as soon as the public power supply failed.

'It sounds like the beginning of a Grand Prix race,' commented one Guyanese friend.

For want of alum at the waterworks the fluid which came out of the taps was the colour of urine. It was often difficult to guess whether you had flushed the lavatory successfully.

With the country's reserves of foreign currency exhausted there was no money for imports. The Guyana Stores, formerly Bookers Stores, the largest department store in the city, to which the plantation company had once brought the world's produce, was a shadow of its former self, its shelves filled with no better a selection of goods than could be found in a similar place in Havana. But, despite the limitations on direct imports everything could be bought. For a consideration some smugglers, big operators or higglers, petty traders, were allowed to bring their goods in through the airport, others with powerful speedboats imported goods from neighbouring Venezuela to the west, others still brought merchandise in from Surinam to the east. In street markets in different parts of Georgetown the contraband trade was openly being carried on on the pavements: food, detergents, electronic goods, anything the ordinary citizen could desire was on offer – at high prices.

The much devalued Guyana dollar itself was traded on the pavements near Tiger Bay for a fraction of its official value. The once highly regarded school system was breaking down. An already underpopulated country was losing people who were emigrating at the rate of 1,000 a month. So high was the rate of emigration that there were too few officials left to run a competent administration – and all too few of those officials who had stayed on were paid enough for them to afford to be honest. The elections had been rigged for decades by a party which represented the negro minority and they would be rigged again.

As a result the majority of Guyanese were at their wits' end with the government. Some of the more conservative and less robust of them were, like Mr Cox, wanting to go back to colonial rule – many people wanted at least to have the benefit of white expertise once more. Some were merely voting with their feet, quitting their country for whatever other country would take them.

On an individual level the people, as Trollope and every modern visitor and expatriate remarked, continued to be the most generous, welcoming, warm hearted and attractive in the West Indies. Politically, the country was putrefying. Guyana, of course, was no Haïti. There was none of the death squad slaughter of Latin American countries as in El Salvador, Guatemala or Argentina, no torture and mass imprisonment of dissidents such as the Chileans suffered under Pinochet, just the decade-long impudence and presumption of a regime which was left reasonably sure that no other government would kick up a fuss if the elections were rigged once again.

'The blacks are motivated by the fear of losing the position of superiority they've conquered over the East Indians: the East Indians are driven by contempt for the mess the blacks have made of running the country,' said one Guyanese friend to me as I set out for Georgetown.

Mary, a black accountant in her late thirties, was my guide to the way in which racialism, fortified and fertilised by the PNC for decades, had taken root in Guyana, even among those who might had been thought to know better. She recounted how her respectable uncle, a successful doctor, had taken her aside one day and asked if her mother knew she had been seen in the company of an East Indian.

On another occasion her grandmother was ill and was consulted as to which doctor should treat her. When one with a very obvious Indian name was suggest she angrily declared,

'Me no' wan' no coolie doctor!'

One of my first calls in Georgetown was on a government official whom I shall call Franco because that was not his name. He had only recently given his support to the PNC government and was all the more avid a supporter for that. He had also made himself indispensible to the regime. As I waited for him to receive me I flicked through the old publications left on the table in the space set aside as the anteroom in Franco's rickety office. One publication was the ridiculous libretto of an opera from North Korea, with which the Guyanese government had close relations. I read it with an increasing sense of incredulity. After scenes of unspeakable bathos the libretto ended with workers, peasants and soldiers singing the everlasting praise of the tyrant Kim Il-Sung.

Eventually I was called in. Franco told me off briskly for the unfavourable things I had written about the PNC and warned me that 'given the bad reputation you've got' it would be difficult for me to speak to any member of the government. I forebore to tell him I felt that, however bad my reputation as a journalist might be, the reputation his government had as a rigger of elections was worse.

In the past, despite the detestation he was held in among the opposition and among many visitors, I had always had a warm spot for Franco. On this meeting my warmth cooled. Self-importance, pomposity and insincerity oozed out of him in equal measures. In an office filled with assorted bureaucratic knick knacks he treated his secretaries, whom he ordered to do this or that peremptorily, with great discourtesy. He epitomized for me the arrogance of a man and a party that had falsified the voting returns and on the basis of the falsifications proclaimed themselves 'paramount' i.e. with the right to interfere and meddle in any citizen's life.

As I left Franco's office I decided to visit the tomb of the man who was the root cause of the problem. Burnham lies in his mausoleum in one of the public gardens of Georgetown. 'Odo' to his intimates, I had met him on my various visits to Guyana and when he was in London. I had seen him at his best and at his worst, presiding over a conference in Georgetown of the Non-Aligned Movement in 1972 and falsifying elections. Once I tackled him on the question of ballot rigging as it concerned the overseas voters. Combining the maximum of mendaciousness with a heavy dose of lordliness he answered,

'It is merely because the People's National Congress has the greater capacity for mobilising the overseas votes that these complaints have arisen . . . I don't see what changes are indicated.'

I had watched him grow old and ill from diabetes. I had seen him at what was perhaps his finest hour in 1983 in Port of Spain when he held out against the majority opinion among Caribbean leaders and condemned the impending US invasion of Grenada. He insisted on calling me 'O'Shuffnessy' – a usage which he presumably based on the way that the word 'enough' is written and pronounced.

He could, like Prime Minister Eric Williams in Trinidad, have opted to weld the races in his country into one nation. Instead, tragically, he made up his mind to keep the blacks ahead of the East Indians. I should have foreseen that tricks and frauds would one day bring his country low.

The body of the maker and the unmaker of his country had for a few days after his death been on show in Georgetown. But the exhibition was called off when the refrigeration, subject to the uncertainties of the city's power supply failed. The body of the great man was then to have been preserved with all the undertaking skills at Moscow's command and thereafter exhibited to the public in a glass coffin rather as Lenin's body is exhibited to the public in Red Square. But something went wrong again in Moscow and the body was shipped back to Georgetown. Today it lies in the coffin, sealed with a concrete plinth. The outside of the plinth is studded with lumps of glass, intended perhaps as a way of allowing party officials to claim that he is indeed in a glass coffin. There is no reference in the inscription to any afterlife for this unyielding atheist.

As I returned to my hotel at the end of Main Street a member of the staff took me aside and murmured that the police had called that morning checking on where I was staying.

On another occasion I went to visit the Jesuits at their white painted wooden presbytery in Brickdam opposite the Catholic cathedral. Sitting mute on the ground, his back resting against the priests' front door, was a handsome black man of about thirty with the dreadlocks of a Rastafarian, dressed in rags, his trousers open to reveal his private parts.

For some reason of ecclesiastic bureaucracy for which the Guyanese should be eternally thankful, the English province of the Jesuit order was given British Guiana as a mission field, and for decades the talented spiritual brethren of Gerard Manley

Hopkins have been travelling to Georgetown and into the interior to bring the gospel to the Guyanese. Several Guyanese themselves followed the demanding path set out by Francis Xavier and Ignatius Loyola and themselves became Jesuits. To their great credit the small Jesuit community became a painful thorn in the side of the People's National Congress. They paid for it with incessant harassment and with one martyrdom. Burnham's thugs murdered Father Bernard Darke, an amateur photographer who was taking pictures of a pro-Burnham demonstration.

I had met two of the Jesuits, Father Robert Barrow and Father Andrew Morrison, on previous visits to Georgetown on my wanderings in other parts of the Caribbean. Bob Barrow, tall, well-built and with a shock of wiry white hair, had been the superior of the little community in Guyana and exuded the sort of uncomplicated and unpretentious friendliness which the relatively small community of catholics in England demands of pastors. Andy Morrison, though equally friendly, was an older figure who combined a gaunt physical aspect with the eagerness of a young reporter keen to do well in his job. His life seemed to be marked by exhilaration. His clerical collar, when he wore it, hung round his scrawny neck like a hoopla ring in some fairground stall and his clothes graced him in the same way that clothes grace a scarecrow.

The rumour was that he had been considered as a candidate to become bishop of Georgetown and might have been named had he only been a native-born Guyanese. He was the particular target of the government for he was the editor of the *Catholic Standard*. The *Standard*, as the masthead week by week announced, was established in 1905 and must in its long history have carried yards of the intemperate conservatism that characterized the Catholic church before the Second Vatican Council. Now it was a scrappily produced eight-page weekly printed on muddy paper the size of a handbill and its regular revelations and denunciations of the government's misdeeds year after year enraged the PNC.

One typical number contained the following items:

'One must give top marks to the ruling group for the care and sophistication displayed in devising the system for

151

rigging, embodied in the Representation of the People Act',

reported 'Cassandra' in a column entitled 'The Rigging of Elections'.

In the anonymous leader in the adjoining column the *Standard* said,

'Visiting Canadian Non-governmental Organisations last year were appalled at the conditions they found in Guyana.'

On the front page a report on police malpractice recounted,

'A watchman at John Fernandes Ltd wharf on Water Street was beaten up by two members of the Quick Reaction Squad at his workplace . . . One of the policemen came up and tapped him on the shoulder and told him to come to the van, allegedly saying, "We gon show you s . . . a thing or two. We gon lock you up. We run things around here."'

On the back page 'Analyst', ironically commenting on the way the opposition's financial policy had been adopted by the PNC, pictured the Minister of Finance,

'comfortable in his armchair dictating his Budget with the *Catholic Standard* of February 18, as his main reference document. It was as easy as that!'

In the letters column 'Old Timer' writing on allegations by Senator Edward Kennedy about crooked elections suggested,

'The President should acknowledge that he is the head of a Government that lacks conclusive legality and he must put his house in order. Fresh, clean elections, adequately monitored by outsiders, will put all the allegations to bed, and if his party wins, the leader will be acknowledged as the legally elected Head of State'.

Finally, there was the weekly front page account of the most notable people who had left the country.

The party for its part had sued the *Catholic Standard*, banned it, cut off its supply of paper, forbade it to accept gifts of paper and murdered Father Bernard Darke, who was a staff member. It had won international recognition and a prize from the Columbia University Graduate School of Journalism in New York. Andy Morrison ensured its continuation, producing a mixture of Christian spiritual uplift, Philippic and news the Government would rather not see printed.

Andy offered me lunch at the presbytery. The untidy common room was littered with newspapers and magazines and contained a well worn library of theological volumes and popular paperbacks. The chicken and salad was followed by jelly and ice cream. If the homely food was reminiscent of some boy's boarding school in England the conversation sparkled with the latest news about town. I was grilled about the political future of Margaret Thatcher. From the wooden wall the photograph of Bernard Darke looked down.

As I left the Rasta was still sitting comfortably against the front door. He never seemed to leave the spot all the time I was in Georgetown.

The Jesuits were not the only religious order to be on bad terms with the government. All my Guyanese friends said I should visit Bishop George, the head of the Anglican church. Mrs George received me with charm in the elegant first drawing room of the wooden palace. The atmosphere in the big, high ceilinged and comfortably furnished Victorian salon looking on to a well kept garden, was no less august than in any of the episcopal palaces in the older cathedral cities of England. It was in strong contrast to the breezy untidiness of the Jesuits. Randolph George himself was a tall, imposing black patrician whose gravitas did full credit to the more formal traditions of Canterbury.

But Randolph George was no stuffed shirt. He had, with the more retiring Catholic bishop, Benedict Singh, criticized the government in forthright terms and had supported the various human rights and reform movements which had surfaced in Guyana. In conversation George was cutting about the practices of the PNC.

'Over the years there has been so much unnecessary suffering inflicted on our people which they should not have tolerated', he said. 'But people are getting together to sweep away things that keep our people down.'

The Jesuits and Bishop George formed a nucleus of opposition to the Hoyte government. This nucleus included two barristers, Miles Fitzpatrick, who had been a legal adviser to Maurice Bishop in Grenada, David de Caries, editor of the *Stabroek News* and Mike McCormack, British born but married to Merle, a Guyanese. Also in the group were N K Gopaul, an East Indian trade union leader and Abdool Azeez, an Islamic teacher. This group was the butt of continual attacks by the government. The PNC seemed to be more concerned about it than about its old enemy the PPP. It was certainly more worried about it than about the Working People's Alliance, a 'new-left' group which had split with Jagan's narrow Muscovite Marxism-Leninism. The WPA leader, the scholar Walter Rodney, had met a violent death in mysterious circumstances in 1980.

The Jesuits and Bishop George were by no means the first clergy to cause problems for the authorities in Georgetown. The great Demerara Revolt of the black slaves in 1823 was blamed on the Reverend John Smith of the London Missionary Society. His nonconformist superiors in England had not sent him to the Demerara to make trouble and had given him strict instructions. Warning of the suspicion of the plantation owners and enjoining him against radicalism the Society ordered,

'Not a word must escape you in public or private, which might render the slaves displeased with their masters or dissatisfied with their station. You are not sent to relieve them from their servile condition, but to afford them the consolations of religion.'

Smith arrived in the colony in 1817 and made a name for himself at his Bethel chapel preaching to the slaves of whom he attracted up to 800 every Sunday. (Some of his congregation must have belonged to John Gladstone, the father of the future British prime minister, who in 1834 owned more than 1,300 slaves worth £70,000 in British Guiana.)

The bolder ones in the congregation used Smith's services to plot. They were particularly incensed at the decision of the governor, Major-General John Murray, not to publish a dispatch from London in which the government announced its intention of progressively dismantling slavery and advising that women slaves should no longer be subject to whipping. An uprising broke out on 18 August 1823 which in a few days had embraced 13,000 slaves. While a small force of regulars, marines and militia under the command of a Captain Muddle was left to guard Georgetown, a field force of 300 including black troops of the First West India Regiment went out to face 2,000 rebels. The troops met the men who were armed with little more than cutlasses or home-made pikes at a plantation called Batchelor's Adventure. The rebels had no chance. More than 100 were killed for the loss of one bugler dead and one rifleman wounded.

Later that year Smith was court-martialled and on 19 November sentenced to be hanged, though his judges recommended mercy. The consumptive Smith was held in prison and on 14 February 1824 George IV ordered him to be reprieved and deported. It was too late: he had died on 6 February. He did not, however, die in vain. He became known as the Demerara Martyr and his story added fuel to the arguments of the abolitionists who achieved emancipation in 1834.

After a few days in Georgetown I was longing to leave the city for Essequibo or the Berbice River and to recapture, however fleetingly, a feeling of what the atmosphere in the country had been like in the old days, a big empty space with gold and diamonds and other unknown and untapped resources which was waiting to be opened up, a place of infinitely more promise and potential than any of the tight little islands in the Caribbean Sea.

That American sense of promise in Guyana had survived until comparatively recently. Mary said she could remember when people from all over the Caribbean, but specially from Barbados, had wanted to come to Guyana to make their fortunes. 'Now,' she added bitterly, 'West Indian immigration officers don't want to let Guyanese into their countries lest they settle permanently there.'

In the sixteenth century the Essequibo was thought to be one of the routes to El Dorado, the mythical kingdom of gold to which European governments, adventurers and explorers were drawn. In his *Discoverie of the Large, Rich and Bewtiful Empire of Guiana with a relation of the great and golden citie of*

Manoa (which the Spaniards call El Dorado) Sir Walter Raleigh urged Queen Elizabeth to found an empire to stretch from the Amazon to the Orinoco.

In 1596 one of Raleigh's captains, Laurence Keymis, sailed up the Essequibo and claimed he had found the lake on which Manoa was supposed to be built, but it was just a flash flood in the savannah. Years later, it was to the Essequibo that the Pilgrim Fathers had considered emigrating before sailing to New England.

John Willems gave me an opportunity to see the broader Guyana outside Georgetown. I had met him briefly at the airport when he came to collect Tom Aitken, the timber buyer. Now he offered to fly me in his little Cessna from Georgetown to the timber concession his company had been granted between the Cuyuni and the Mazaruni Rivers on the other side of the Essequibo.

Trollope's sugar barons had disappeared from Guyana but had they been alive they would have recognized John Willems' spirit of enterprise as their own. John Willems, a man of Belgian and East Indian ancestry, employed 500 men in one of the biggest timber operations in a country whose forests are capable of producing great quantities of timber. But now he feared that the ecological lobby in Europe which was alleging that the forest was being despoiled of its best hardwoods, would impose a boycott of his products. He wanted to demonstrate to me that rare species like greenheart were not being annihilated but were reproducing themselves in the forest.

Leaving the city behind we crossed the Demarara and within minutes were heading south-west over a mixture of brilliant green swamp and dark green jungle. To the inexperienced eye of a passenger in an aeroplane neither the swamp nor the jungle showed any sign of human hand beyond the occasional path and tiny and isolated cleared patch in the forest.

'All this so near Georgetown,' John Willems said, 'has been well and truly exploited.'

He piloted his small aircraft through the clouds and over the wilderness. With the help of the compass, of an occasional contact over the crackling radio and of his own intimate knowledge of the ground he navigated with all the assurance of a Londoner shopping in Regent Street. In forty minutes we sighted the Esse-

quibo stretching out near the end of its 600 mile length like a sea
in front of us. We crossed it and I watched a power boat speed-
ing along like some aquatic daddy-longlegs leaving its wake
across the deserted river. On the other side we picked up the
trace of a road which had been constructed by Burnham to allow
access to the site of a huge dam, a Guyanese Aswan, which he
had wanted to build on the upper waters of the Mazaruni River.
He never could persuade the banks to allow him to borrow
enough to finance it and this road to nowhere was the only monument to his efforts.

John put the plane down through the trees on to a bumpy dirt
strip beside the road and in a moment his overseer, Nazeem
Khan, and Tom, who was on a tour of inspection of the wood
which would eventually be sent to his Scottish yard, appeared in
a truck to take us into the forest.

The forest that morning was still, beautiful and majestic. The
tops of the biggest trees were lost to view amid the greenery, and
the lianas fell like strings and ropes from the branches. From
time to time the silence was broken by the bell-like call of a bird.

'The foresters call it the greenheart bird because its call always
leads you to a greenheart,' said John. He added sceptically, 'But
the gold miners call the same bird the gold bird because its call is
supposed to lead you to gold.'

The walk in the forest was memorable, too, for the intimate
way in which Nazeem Khan and his men seemed to know every
tree in the forest, which to fell and which to leave. John's company had cleared tracks through the trees to allow the timber to
be taken out, but they were no more than deeply rutted
thoroughfares interrupted by pools and puddles. We drove five
miles along the tracks to where John was keen to show me the
thriving greenheart saplings.

On the way we picked up a group of four foresters, ragged,
taciturn, expert men who worked for Khan. Like gardeners in
some giant nursery they knew which were the diseased trees,
which were the valuable trees and which would make good telegraph poles. With the care and ease of surgeons using scalpels
they demonstrated how they used their power saws to cut down a
tree and in a few minutes to fashion it into a telegraph pole. Here
and there we came across old stumps eight feet high. They reminded the present generation of foresters of the labour of their

ancestors. A generation ago foresters had no other tools but big hand saws and they had to build scaffoldings round the trees they wanted to fell so that they would have a thinner trunk to cut through. More recent stumps of trees felled with power saws were much closer to the ground. Despite their rags the foresters looked supremely at home and content in the forest.

John, anxious to demonstrate his concern for greenhearts, hurried us on. Greenhearts, of which there were only about one to an acre, liked well drained slopes. The foresters could spot a slope in what to my untrained eye looked impenetrable jungle and we soon found a glade with three or four saplings growing. John was triumphant: here was living proof that he was not just pillaging the forest.

We bumped back through the silent forest to the airstrip and took off for Kaow Island, the heart of John Willems' operations, his own little kingdom. We circled to the south to fly down the Essequibo over magnificent sets of rapids studded with islands. We passed the town of Bartica handsomely sited at the point where the Mazaruni and the Cuyuni flow into the Essequibo, each of the three rivers of a size which would dwarf virtually every river in Europe. A mile or two downstream from Bartica we put down on the island.

Neither Ian Fleming nor Alexandre Dumas could do justice to Kaow Island and neither, I suppose, shall I. The island lies in the middle of the river, a mile of brown water separating it from each bank and on it the Willems family built their realm.

This was the spot from which the original Dutch settlers hoped to build their Guianese empire, the site of Fort Kykoveral.

The island is a mile or so long and a third of a mile wide. At the southern tip stood a mill full of sawdust and the savage saws capable of reducing the biggest tree in the forest to planks. It was all powered from the electricity produced from the steam of a hissing, ancient boiler into whose roaring red mouth the boiler-men stuffed the useless offcuts of wood. Beside the mill stood a dock for the ferryboat from Bartica and the barges which brought the tree trunks in and took the sawn lumber away.

A few hundred yards away stood the modern house, built on stilts in the finest hardwood, in which the family could live when they were not in Georgetown and on whose side verandas and in whose plentiful bedrooms they could entertain their guests. Tom Aitken and I sat with John on wooden chairs on the veranda, sipped our drinks and looked down, past the little jetty, where a speedboat was tied up, to the Essequibo. One could easily imagine why the Dutch picked such a spot. It was easy to defend but had enough depth of water to harbour the biggest ships sent out from Amsterdam with goods to trade with the Indians and which took back to Amsterdam cotton, dies, woods and sugar.

The trip to the Essequibo raised my spirits. By reminding me of the size of Guyana it demonstrated that under better political management the Guyanese would have everything they needed to make a prosperous and human society in their vast country.

A few weeks after I left Guyana the Government's newspaper, the *New Nation*, published a long article under the title 'O'Shaughnessy – Morrison mischief-making doomed to failure'. Criticizing an article I had written about Guyana, it started,

'That old foe of Guyana – the pseudo writer, Hugh O'Shaughnessy, is at it again. . . . It will be recalled that, for years, O'Shaughnessy, instigated by Father Morrison, has been peddling misinformation about Guyana . . . But then, what is to be expected from Morrison's hired gun?'

I sensed the hand of Franco in the piece: I felt flattered that he had called me Andy Morrison's hired gun.

Chapter Seven

Surinam

'Hotels and restaurants are rare outside the capital, and you usually have to bring your own hammock and mosquito net, and food.'

South American Handbook, 1990

'I'll have a beer, please. A Heineken.'

The barman at the Hotel Torarica laughed.

'No. You'll have a Parbo. We haven't seen no Heineken here for a long while.'

There was no foreign currency for imported beers in Holland's former colony of Surinam and the best hotel in Paramaribo was exhibiting that combination of unkemptness and emptiness that characterizes all luxury hotels in newly revolutionary countries.

Though the sun was hot the pool was almost empty of people, the upholstery was fraying and there was little or nothing to buy at the kiosk. It was reminiscent of the erstwhile Havana Hilton in the Cuban capital and the Managua Inter-Continental in Nicaragua. (Luxury hotels in revolutionary countries present problems to their governments. They are needed to accommodate distinguished foreign delegations but they are looked at askance by the revolutionaries who see in them echoes of the *ancien régime* and who correctly suspect them of being nests of black marketers, illegal currency dealers and traffickers in unobtainable motor spares.)

Such, anyway, was the fate of the Torarica under the rule of Colonel Désiré (Desi) Bouterse. Bouta, as he is known to his friends and enemies, seized power at the beginning of 1980.

160

Since then he has steered a wobbly left-wing course, now accepting Dutch handouts, now cursing the hated imperialists; now courting the Cubans and the Libyans, now distancing himself from them. The only constant was that authority in this massive tropical wilderness, wedged on the north-east flank of South America between Brazil and the Atlantic Ocean, should remain in the sinewy hands of the former sergeant-major and physical training instructor in the Dutch army. He was facing an equally wobbly guerrilla opposition.

The teeming streets of the city tell of the intricate racial history of Surinam. The people, no more than about 400,000 in a country the size of Britain, are of all colours. The original people were an Amerindian tribe called the Surinas who were later joined by Arawak from the Caribbean. The first European settlers, in what was for a time known as Willoughbyland, were the English. They arrived in 1630 and a colony was formally established in 1650 by a magnate of the time, Lord Willoughby of Parham, governor of the overcrowded island of Barbados. In 1667 under the Peace of Breda the English pulled off the most unequal real estate deal ever, swapping Willoughbyland with the Dutch for New Amsterdam, later known as New York.

The Dutch held it from them on, with short breaks of English and French occupation, till 1975. The burghers of Amsterdam controlled it through high-sounding bodies of state such as the *Committee tot de Zaken van de Koloniën en bizittingen op de kust van Guinea en in Amerika* (the Administrative Committee for the Colonies and Possessions on the Coasts of Guinea and in America) and the *Raad voor het Bestuur van de West-Indische Bezittingen en Koloniën in Amerika en op de Kust van Guinea* (the Administrative Council for the West Indian Possessions and Colonies in America and on the Coasts of Guinea).

They brought in labour from around the world to till the sugar cane fields and run the colony. The Dutch cultivated intensely a narrow strip of flat land along the Atlantic while the mountainous jungle interior was left untouched, as it is today. Jews, blacks and Germans came and Portuguese and Chinese.

As a business – and Surinam like most colonies was essentially a business venture – it never really recovered from the double blow that hit it towards the end of the last century. In 1863, long after the rest of Europe had abolished slavery, the Dutch set free the 33,000 slaves working on their Surinamese plantations. They were forced to labour another ten years in the fields under contract but then a new and more expensive labour force had to be found as they drifted away from the plantations. The Dutch then recruited 34,000 coolies from British India. Finally the Dutch started importing workers from their own East Indian colonies, notably Javanese. As a result few Surinamers have the blood of only one race in their veins.

Six years after emancipation came another disaster for the Dutch colonialists. In 1869 the Suez Canal opened and cheapened greatly the cost of Asian tropical products in the European market. Cane sugar from Surinam, which was already facing stiff competition from European sugar beet, and other products from the colony, were hard hit.

In 1875 a gold rush began in the Lawa district in the interior and a hopeful company undertook to build a railway into the jungle in exchange for mining rights over the most promising 500,000 hectares. In the end the company failed, the railway was never built and the Surinam government lost millions of guilders bailing the enterprise out.

Ironically in the light of the vast sums the Dutch were eventually to spend in launching the country into independence, there was in 1910 a plot hatched by a Hungarian police inspector called Kilinger and some cronies to declare Surinam a republic, pay compensation to the Netherlands for the loss and raise a loan for new capital ventures on the international market. Unluckily for the Netherlands the plotters were unmasked and arrested.

In 1972 the Dutch decided they would leave Surinam to its own devices, independence and the mercies of the Surinamers' own squabbling political parties. There were a great number of them with names like Verenigde Hindostaanse Partij, or Kaum-Tani Persuatan Indonesia or Progressieve Surinaamse Volkspartij which claimed to represent the tiny slivers of browns, blacks, yellows, whites, the left, the right, the rich, the poor in the already minute population. For five years these racial parties struggled to spend the enormous payoff the government in The Hague had given them in a fit of conscience about its colonialist past. The result was a deal of good-humoured chaos and corruption.

Then along came Sergeant-Major Bouterse, army rule and

revolution and things changed drastically. The corrupt decadent civilian politicians were replaced by Bouta and his friends, some of whom are decadent, not a few corrupt and one or two outrightly savage. The flower of the opposition, fifteen leading politicians, trade unionists, lawyers, journalists and academics, were shot on 8 December 1982.

The Bouta regime struggled towards some sort of Third World ideological underpinning for its actions, both for the understandable ones like trying to forge a new sense of nationhood, distinct from the Dutch, among people of such varied racial and cultural backgrounds, and for the unforgivable ones, like massacring the opposition. It did not have much success.

The empty mottoes told all: 'Labour is the Architect and Defender of Sovereignty', 'Organize and Unite', 'The History of Labour is the History of our Culture', 'Surinam: A Corner Stone . . . a rock hard muscle of one shoulder of our America'. In a country where the government has been long on rhetoric and short on any sort of profound social change the revolution was what Bouta said it was.

Revolution or no revolution, Paramaribo – Parbo to its friends – remained what it had been for centuries, a place of amazing elegance, a tropical Amsterdam full of the loveliest architectural monuments to Holland's colonial sojourn in the New World. Unvisited by tourists and unknown to the outside world, the Surinamese capital has few rivals in America for the beauty of its buildings.

Broad tree-shaded boulevards, Gravenstraat, Heerenstraat, Keizerstraat and the incomparable Waterkant overlooking the Surinam River, were lined with the great white mansions in brick and wood of the eighteenth-century Dutch colonial planters and traders, the colonnades and verandas soberly picked out with carved wooden lintels and elegant wrought iron work. The patrons of architecture and their craftsmen clearly vied among themselves as to who could combine the greatest degree of elegance and delicacy with the highest quality of inventiveness.

The Surinamese foreign ministry, for instance, is now lodged in Number 6 Gravenstraat, a magnificent two-storey palace with cellar and mansard. It was put up in 1774 for the Governor Jean Nepveu and later on became a masonic temple of the Concordia lodge. Its great windows, curving staircase and finely moulded

wood give an overpowering sense of the wealth and the graciousness of the lives of the tiny white minority who benefited from
the labour of so many slaves.

The Lutheran and the Reformed churches vied in beauty with
the synagogues with the prize surely going to the serenely classical Portuguese synagogue Sedek ve Salom dating back to 1736.
There are even one or two canals and sluices left from when the
Dutch used to fuss around with the water.

Down the road in the shopping streets crowded, it seems, with
people from all the races of the world, the feeling was more
robust. There was a massive covered market where stall holders
sold every household essential, a garish Chinese club with a massive pagoda-like gateway and a mosque with onion domes which
seem to be made out of papier-mâché. Because of the lack of
foreign currency the stores were pretty empty of goods and the
assistants were listless. But the goldsmiths and jewellers,
Chinese and Indians mostly, fashioning an infinity of different
bangles and brooches from the lustrous orange-coloured gold
that the rivers of the interior yield up, did a roaring trade. With a
worthless currency, Surinamers who could afford it put their
faith in gold. The cinemas warned patrons that they would not
get their money back if a power cut put an end to the per-
formance.

In the intense heat the traveller's refuge was the Alegría, an
open-air ice cream parlour, or the Palmentuin, a shady grove of
massive palm trees where from time to time Parbo's whores
gently trawled for work.

'O'Shaughnessy, eh?' said Ambassador Henk Heidweiller.

'I will arise and go now, and go to Innisfree,
And a small cabin build there, of clay and wattles made;
Nine bean rows will I have there, and a hive for the honey
bee,
And live alone in the bee-loud glade.'

I had not expected to be greeted in Fort Zeelandia with the
poetry of William Butler Yeats by Bouta's right-hand man but
there ensued a long and interesting discussion about whether the
great Irish writer was indeed a crypto-fascist. Heidweiller was a

widely read and intelligent man, grey-haired and of mature years, the most civilized, they said, of those who surrounded the ruler of Surinam. The building in which Heidweiller had his office started as Fort Willoughby in the time of the English. Later it was the bastion of the Dutch against marauders. Over the centuries it acquired that old world charm which in Europe makes one forget the torture, blood and misery attaching to many of our old castles. In Rotterdam or Eindhoven it would have been a tourist attraction where parents would take their children for summer picnics. It was not a tourist attraction in Paramaribo. Firstly there were no tourists in Surinam: secondly memories were too fresh of the day when the fifteen were executed within its walls. With its pretty shingle roofs, eighteenth-century cannons and mellow brick, Fort Zeelandia today was a place you passed with a shudder and sat in with apprehension. In the quiet courtyard stood a couple of Brazilian armoured cars.

Having disposed of Yeats, the ambassador argued passionately and at length that there was nothing that Colonel Bouterse wanted more than free elections and an end to the civil war which had been raging in the interior for a year.

Yes, there were Libyans in Surinam. It was a normal embassy but, no, they presented no threat to the country's neighbours or to the stability of the region. The bush negroes led by the Colonel's former bodyguard Corporal Ronny Brunswijk who had revolted against the government were no more than a band of ruffians who did not know what they wanted.

I left the fort and crossed Independence Square (or to give it its sonorous Dutch name Onafhankelijkheidsplein), a great lawn surrounded by elegant colonnaded buildings. Had it not been for the broiling sun it could have been the centre of any historic Dutch city. Near the market there was a small anti-Bouta riot going on. The uniformed police with wicker shields were nervously putting up with the taunts of the older schoolchildren while plain clothes thugs chased off any adult who attempted to join the children.

It was easy to know when you were coming to the rapids. You looked ahead and the river was a foot or two above you pouring smoothly over the rocks with scarcely a splash. At the prow of the canoe, a vessel hewn out of the trunk of some massive forest tree, the navigator stood, small pole in one hand, signalling with deft wrist movements to the man at the outboard motor on the stern the best path between the eddies. The craft, full of drums of petrol, sacks of rice and a dozen passengers wove upstream like a snake. The grace and intelligence of man were pitted against the power of nature.

Four hours upriver from the French town of Saint-Laurent the Marowijne was still nearly a mile across. The sun was pitiless to a northern European skin. I had buttoned up the cuffs of my shirt to protect my forearms from the blaze and covered the backs of my hands with oil. In vain. Still I was burning. Eventually I sat on my glistening hands to keep them from being seared and protected my head by creeping under the plastic mackintosh which I had originally bought at the Chinese supermarket at Saint-Laurent to keep off tropical downpours. I was still badly sunburnt.

On both banks the heavy tropical vegetation spilt over into the river, the occasional human settlements being all but hidden behind curtains of greenery. On the left was Guyane or French Guiana. A mile or two back we had passed Apatou, a small village with a gendarmerie, a thatched hut surmounted by an enormous tricolour proclaiming to men, monkeys and parrots alike that the writ of Paris and the French Republic ran in this area of dense South American jungle. The right bank was Surinam. It was in the hands of the bush negroes fighting the Bouta government in Paramaribo.

Every twenty minutes or so our canoe would put into some small settlement on the French side, a long-standing bush negro village or a group of one or two huts tucked like a bird's nest between the mangroves at the water's edge and the giant trees of the forest. Occasionally we would come across a newer foundation, recently slashed out of the jungle, home for refugees from the fighting in Surinam. At each stop a passenger or two would get out with a basket, a baby or a bundle, lightening the load and allowing our hollowed out log to scud more daintily over the water.

The bush negroes are one of the most remarkable of the races of Surinam. They descend from the slaves who ran away from the Dutch plantations over the centuries and set up their own societies in the jungle ruled over by their leaders, the *grand-*

mans. They are little known but feared in Parbo. When the young Brunswijk broke with Bouta in 1986 and decided to oppose him it was to his own race he had recourse. Slowly and hesitatingly and with little money or arms a 'Jungle Commando' was put together which carried out acts of sabotage against the Bouta government and its army from bases deep in the jungle. Some funds came from the large but bitterly divided Surinamese community in the Netherlands. The French, having no reason to love Bouta, his Third World rhetoric or the Libyan presence in Surinam which might one day menace the European space station at Kourou in Guyane, turned a blind eye to the use of Guyane as a safe haven and resupply base for the Jungle Commando. The French became even more closely involved when, after Bouta's forces had killed a group of Surinamese bush negroes, refugees fled from the forests of Surinam across the river to their kin on French territory.

Between 5,000 and 10,000 people from Surinam were in French refugee camps or living rough in the forests of Guyane. Like refugee camps worldwide the ones in Guyane were centres of unrest, difficulty and intrigue where people had to be fed, housed and clothed for nothing. A well-built black youth of twenty in our canoe confessed that he was going back to the Jungle Commando to fight Bouta.

By five o'clock the pitiless sun lost some of its strength. Silhouetted on the horizon were the jungle-covered mountain ranges which had scarely been trodden by the white man or by human beings of any race for that matter. With passengers and cargo being dropped off at nearly every jungle clearing the canoe was considerably lighter as we raced for our destination. As the sun began to drop the Jungle Commandos' Base Number One came into view. A big wooden jetty had the word *LANGATAB-BETJE* carefully painted in foot-high letters over it as though it were some important town on a railway line in Holland. Erwin Macdonald, Brunswijk's lieutenant, a massive black who spent years as a social worker among the Surinamese community in the Netherlands and whose mountainous bulk was with difficulty contained in a shirt and a pair of shorts, was there to meet me with a broad smile.

'Welcome to Base Number One,' he said.

A nondescript bunch of blacks each wearing one or other bit of uniform unloaded the rice and condensed milk left in the canoe and took them into the forlorn wooden buildings which until a year or two previously housed a mission school on what is an island three or four miles long in the middle of the Marowijne and the territory of the Republic of Surinam.

'Before we have anything to eat and while there still is some light I want to show you something,' said Macdonald eagerly. Past the deserted classrooms we went through the long grass till we came to a rough landing strip. Sitting on the strip were two small airliners. They had been there for months, trophies of war. After my departure they netted Brunswijk's men a lot of money from the insurers from London who were finally allowed to have them flown away. As we returned to the mission school one of Macdonald's men tugged urgently at my sleeve.

'You will find some weapons for us, won't you? If we had a rifle each we could be in Parbo in a week.'

I made sympathetic but noncommital noises.

The headquarters was sparse. A map of Surinam was on the wall and stuck beside it a drawing of two gladiators, one on the ground and about to be dispatched by the other. The caption read, 'Ronny kill Bouta'.

On a blotter on the school desk was a rubber stamp bearing the words 'Jungle Commando'. In another classroom there was a radio linking Langatabbetje with Ronny's headquarters at Stoel-manseiland hours away up the Marowijne. I was not taken to see it and I suspected that it was not at the peak of efficiency.

As night fell Macdonald took me to the living quarters of the commando leaders by way of the bush negro village beside the old mission on Langatabbetje. Outside palm-thatched huts bare-breasted women pounded manioc roots in primitive wooden mortars to make rough flour and chaffed the guerrillas with whom they were obviously on good terms.

The leaders' quarters were in a two-storey wooden house a few yards from the Marowijne.

'There is no electricity and the water comes from the river. That's all we can offer,' said Macdonald graciously. 'You'll be quite safe, Bouta can't get at us here. I would like you to sleep in my room with me and my bodyguard. Would you prefer the bed or the hammock? The lavatory is in that hut over there.'

I opted for the bed and pondered on the fact that I had received much less cordial receptions in the past at Holiday Inns.

Over supper of a delicious vegetable soup, made with the brown water of the Marowijne, and a stew, I grilled the guerrillas about their political objectives and got no very clear answer.

'We going to overthrow Bouta. We going to put back democracy,' was the refrain. 'You will help us to get more guns, won't you?' The young Ronny, still in his mid-twenties, Macdonald and the jungle commando's advisers among the warring Surinamese opposition factions still living in Holland were clearly not getting very far in agreeing on a political platform beyond that of ousting the government in Paramaribo.

'It's good you come to see us here fighting. A lot of Bouta's enemies who live in comfortable houses in Amsterdam haven't dared come here,' one of Ronny's men said bitterly.

After supper the guerrillas crowded round my short-wave radio to hear the news in Dutch from Holland, clearly a rare experience for them. As it ended they eagerly dissected the political report from Paramaribo. The Surinamese capital could have been on the other side of the world, rather than a hundred miles or so through the jungle, for all the direct contact we had with it here at Langatabbetje.

Each of the men wore an amulet of some sort, either a piece of knotted red cloth on a string round the neck or a piece of copper wire twisted round the upper forearm.

'These things are our spirit protection. It means that Bouta's bullets can never hurt us. The Obeah man makes them for us,' said Macdonald. Several guerrillas told long stories with utter conviction about how their own lives had been saved from enemy attack by the spirits working through the cloth or the wire.

I enjoyed an excellent night's rest at Langatabbetje, stirring only to see some shadowy figure leaving the house to go on guard duty. As six o'clock dawn burst, the camp came alive and a canoe awaited Macdonald and me. He had to inspect a detachment of guerrillas on a tiny island guarding the downstream approach to the base beside the rapids. I had passed them the previous afternoon without noticing them.

Dawn on the Marowijne was exceptionally dramatic. The stillness was total till it was broken by the roar of our outboard starting up. The air was cool, the water warm and glassy calm and the mist, not yet dispelled by the rays of the sun, hung over the river like a series of silken veils obscuring the distant banks. Thrust forward by our whining motor the canoe, loaded with rice and tins for the men, shot along like a torpedo boat, guided by a black steersman who navigated calmly through our misty isolation as though by some infallible radar. No stage set for a Wagner opera, neither *The Twilight of the Gods* nor *The Flying Dutchman*, was ever more dramatic.

As the sun came up we reached the tiny island, scarcely twenty-five yards across but covered with big forest trees, in the middle of the whirlpools. The garrison of Tapoe Dang, a dozen, mostly teenagers armed with a few old rifles and small bores, were clearly delighted to see us and formed a primitive guard of honour as we jumped from the canoe. Macdonald delivered the condensed milk, rice and an encouraging chat and within half an hour we were on our way back upstream.

'What would happen if Bouta's men really did attack them?' I asked Macdonald.

'They would fire a series of warning shots and the villagers on the bank would relay the message up to us by firing their own shots,' said the guerrilla commander. 'And we'd come down and drive Bouta's men away.'

Primitive communications for a primitive war.

On the way back to Langatabbetje we put into a little riverside village, Soela Tapoe, for a late breakfast. Soela Tapoe was a collection of thatched huts round a small cove where naked children were playing in the water and women were washing clothes. The village chief, Humphrey Bodo, was an Obeah man who was clearly intensely loyal to Brunswijk and whose skill, making effective amulets, was much sought after by the Jungle Commando. He was son-in-law to one of the most venerable grandmans of the region and highly regarded by Macdonald.

'Without this man and the power he has brought us from the spirits we would have lost a lot more men,' said Macdonald. He talked in deadly earnest. 'Our fighters can pick whichever Obeah man they want but he is mine and he's the best,' said Macdonald with proprietorial pride.

Seated in wicker chairs beside the river where the naked village children splashed and played we consumed mashed sardines and boiled rice washed down with rum and water from a freshly cut coconut.

Humphrey, an intelligent and well-informed man, gave his views on apartheid, which he detested, and Jesus Christ, in whom he believed. Bush negroes' magic, he argued, was better even than the original African magic of his distant ancestors. With compelling logic and acute historical sense he pointed out that had African magic been up to standard blacks would never have been sold into slavery and dispatched to the New World all those centuries ago. Helped by the spirits in Surinam his people had been living free in the forests for generations – and intended to continue to do so.

As for the amulets, the powers of plants and spirits could, as it were, be distilled into them and the commandos who wore them could therefore benefit by them. Spirits could be persuaded to pass on messages about the future in dreams.

'This man has foretold six attacks by Desi Bouterse,' Macdonald butted in enthusiastically. 'Six.'

As the run rose higher Patricia, Humphrey's daughter and a teacher, took our tin plates away. We bade our farewells, climbed into the canoe and were back at Langatabbetje before midday.

The journey back down the Marowijne to Saint-Laurent and to European ways was swift. The canoe was empty of other passengers, there was no freight and we whizzed along in royal style – royal style, that is, but for the fact that I was cowering under a piece of plastic that I pulled round me for protection from a sun whose rays were even hotter than on the journey upstream and which burnt even the exposed tips of my fingers.

As the gaunt wooden convict hospital of Saint-Laurent came in sight I fell to thinking about the future of the bush negroes. Would a race of people who had fled slavery on the plantation to live close to nature in the jungle ever make their peace with the multiplicity of races dwelling in the towns and cities? Could they ever live in the same society with the heirs to the jewellery shops and the fine elegant buildings in the Waterkant of Parbo?

Chapter Eight

The Monaco of the Atlantic

'In a word, 90,000 convicts came to Guyane and created nothing.'

Arthur Henry, *La Guyane Française, son Histoire, 1604-1946*

'**I** gather, *Monsieur le Prefet*, you are leaving for France tonight.'

Sitting in the elegant, cool, wood-panelled office of Jacques Dewatre in the white concrete prefecture of the little town of Cayenne I felt that was a polite and respectful way to start the conversation. Dewatre was after all the senior official in this, France's only *département* on the American continent, the ruler of a vast empty enclave of tropical jungle where the tricolour still flies. His secretary had told me the prefect was flying off that evening for Paris and, please, would I keep to the thirty minutes he had kindly spared me.

Dewatre's response was exact and meticulous.

'I am already in France. Tonight I am merely returning to the metropolis.'

'Yes of course, *excusez-moi*.'

Since 1946 Guyane, Surinam's eastern neighbour, like Guadeloupe and Martinique, has been a *département d'outre-mer*, an overseas department of France, no less France than the Pas de Calais or the Vendée, equal in status to the *départements* into which metropolitan France was divided by Bonaparte after the French Revolution. They have prefects in Lille and Bordeaux, Rennes and Montpelier, so they have one in Cayenne.

For a lot longer than half an hour, Dewatre, a man of culture and broad vision, though rather too authoritarian for his critics, talked of the future of Guyane. For centuries Guyane was a graveyard of dreams, a place for the convicted and the damned, known for Devil's Island and the tragedy of Alfred Dreyfus in the last century: now, as the site of Europe's launch pad into space, the home of the Ariane rocket, it weighs in the world's affairs as never before.

'This place is of vital importance to France and to Europe,' Dewatre said. 'If, for instance, some Libyan firecracker went off in front of 150 journalists attending the launch of Ariane at Kourou it could do enormous harm to Europe's commercial prospects in space. We have to be careful.'

Successive prefects have, it must be said, made little of the job of governing Guyane. The opportunities for economic development in a rugged, underpopulated, jungle-covered stretch of South America with poor soil have never been good. The territory has subsisted on subsidies from Paris. Nothing local has ever succeeded.

'The rest of the French Antilles – Guadeloupe, Martinique and the other islands – look down on Guyane. You see, with the penal colony, this was the only place in the Caribbean where the slaves were white,' my friend Artigalas had told me.

Now the Kourou rocket launching site has given the place some real importance and Dewatre knows he has a real and important job. He has to protect a massive investment on the one hand and on the other to cajole people into tilling the land.

About half Guyane's population of 80,000 live in Cayenne. The town is certainly French. It is a cheerful, scruffy sort of place built on the right bank of the great oil serpentine Cayenne River where it empties its mile-wide load of brown water into the brown Atlantic. There are gendarmes in blue uniforms in the streets, fresh baguettes and croissants for breakfast, surly taxi drivers and *France Soir* and *Le Monde* on sale – albeit a few days late – in the newsagents. The main street is called avenue Charles de Gaulle. Nowhere in the Americas, remarked one visitor, is the influence of the United States less obvious.

But if it's French, it's French with a difference. The midday heat is more intense than anything you experience even in the Midi and it's rare to see anyone in a jacket and tie. And the town is preponderantly black. Half the shops and businesses seem to be owned by Chinese. (On hot afternoons, when the rest of

Cayenne is enjoying its siesta, the Chinese toddlers gather in the Chinese Club, under the Nationalist flag and the benign photograph of Chiang Kai-Shek, to learn and chorus out their pictograms.)

Here and there you catch sight of an Amerindian face. Untraceable in the crowds are thousands of illegal immigrants from Haïti, who have come from the poorest country in the New World attracted by Guyane's comparatively high standard of living and need for workers to do the dirtiest of jobs. Haïtians, content with small wages, sharing the creole language, the version of French spoken in every Caribbean territory which is, or, like Haïti, once was, controlled by France, are ideal imported labour.

But there is an unease under the cheerful scruffiness.

'*C'est pas le bagne*,' they say. 'This isn't the penal colony.' The sufferings of the 90,000 convicts who were transported to France's dumping ground for criminals still hang in the air like some ineradicable tropical miasma over Guyane. For nearly a century, till after the Second World War, disease, exhaustion, solitary confinement and unalloyed despair took the lives of perhaps half the unfortunates who were sent to Guyane. It is not a story which can be lightly forgotten. Cayenne tries to forget it.

The Café des Palmistes is the hub of social life in the town. It overlooks the main square, the Place des Palmistes, whose neatly aligned rows of royal palms give a touch of splendour, the fleetingest touch of Versailles, to this chirpy, unpretentious place.

At tables on the pavement *terrasse* sit the latest crop of hitch-hikers from Europe or newly arrived businessmen from Brazil. At the electronic pin-tables inside crewcut soldiers from the battalion outside town swear and guffaw while at the bar a Vietnamese family with a baby finishes a snack.

The restaurant is the nearest thing that Cayenne gets to the Café des Deux Magots. In it Cayenne's beau monde observe, preen, converse and are seen. One day I went in with a friend. At a table by the door sat Kenneth Middellijn, the young consul of the Republic of Surinam, Guyane's unpredictable left-wing neighbour to the west. Once a fiery medical student and champion of the fight against the colonial Dutch, he was lunching with Jean-Claude Artigalas, a local journalist and the best informed man in Guyane. I waved to them. I had lunched the

174

previous day with Middellijn and dined the evening before with Artigalas.

My companion for lunch was less effusive. The Surinamers had just expelled the Dutch ambassador to Surinam so Alfons Hamer, Queen Beatrix's diplomtic representative in Guyane, did not think it right to be too outgoing to Middellijn. Hamer, a brilliant Oriental scholar who was the eyes and ears of the Dutch embassy in Tehran during the Khomeini revolution, had been drafted down from the Dutch mission at the United Nations to do a diplomatic fireman's job in Guyane while the crisis lasted with Surinam. He wanted to get back to New York and he was not a patient man. But the diplomatic game between the Netherlands and Surinam had to be played out with the full gravity of the princely court of Ruritania. Hamer did not wave to Middellijn. Middellijn did not greet Hamer. The dignity of Queen Beatrix and the honour of the fledgling Republic of Surinam were preserved in the Café des Palmistes. In Cayenne, as in any other capital, the diplomatic life is seen to be made up of the same equal measures of alcohol, vitriol and protocol.

'*Ce n'est plus le bagne*. This country is no longer the penal colony. Tell them that.' The public relations man from the space centre was urgent and pleading. Distancing themselves from history is the first preoccupation of decent citizens in Guyane.

We sit in the Hotel des Roches. Tennis courts, a swimming pool and a thatched open-air restaurant overlook a flat muddy shore and the brown Atlantic. On the horizon through the heat haze you can make out the rocky contour of Devil's Island. Created a penal colony by Emperor Louis-Napoleon in 1854, it was for years home to Captain Dreyfus after he was framed and imprisoned by French anti-semites in the last century, for Papillon and for thousands of others. I have no wish to visit the island. The misery is almost tangible.

But in 1988 the image of Guyane as nothing other than *le bagne* has to be changed. Today it is Kourou, Europe's space centre. The Centre Spatial Guyanais is the home of generations of new space vehicles, the sanctuary in the New World for the scientific aspiration of France and the Old World, a town of whites in a country of blacks. What scientists would want to come and work if they still think it's *le bagne*?

On flat scrubland a mile or two inland behind the town of Kourou and its rows of neat technicians' bungalows lies the Centre overlooked by a satellite communications centre with its parabolic dishes stuck on the top of a big hill. The offices are cool and antiseptic. On the second floor of the headquarters building is the control room, a smaller version of NASA's great installation in Houston, with control consoles, giant TV screens and digital clocks for countdown.

A few miles beyond are the launch sites. The assembly dock of the newer of the two sites is a giant structure for the piecing together of Arianes which are shipped over by boat from France. It is a modern cathedral built to elevate the true presence of the sacred satellite to the tip of the rocket and there to venerate it like some host in its costly medieval monstrance. Within the perimeter the scientists beetle about in a fleet of identical small cars like ants in a Kafkaesque fantasy. The perimeter is of barbed wire.

'Ce n'est plus le bagne, vous savez,' murmurs a technician. He hands me a copy of *Forward to the Future*, a glossy brochure bearing on its cover the map of Europe superimposed arrogantly on a photograph of our galaxy. Outside the headquarters the flags of the Europeans flutter on their masts, most of Western Europe from Ireland to Austria. It is a brave sight.

But the miasma of history has yet to be lifted. Kourou was a disappointing, ill-starred place even before it became a penal colony. Writing in 1731 Père Labat reported that venturers were attracted to Cayenne by the widespread rumour that

'that country was infinitely rich; that gold and silver were as common there as stones; that quarries of Emeralds and other stones of great value were to be found; in a word immense and inexhaustible wealth, which offered itself for the taking, which seemed only to be waiting for vehicles to be taken away and spread to other parts of the world, which it would have infinitely enriched.'

He went on to paint a flattering, probably excessively flattering, picture of colonial life in the town of Cayenne.

'One lives in Cayenne in marvellous comfort; however

modest his resources an Inhabitant always keeps a good table, without leaving his dwelling he finds all that he needs to make his food abundant & delicious. No one lacks a farm-yard in which to keep a few Slaves to look after all sorts of game, & four-footed beasts like cattle, calves, sheep, goats & pigs . . .

'As each inhabitant has his laundresses, the linen there is extremely clean & dazzlingly white. The Negresses are better than all the world's laundresses. I believe that the water has much to do with it, apart from the fact that as table linen is changed at each meal little has to be done to make it white . . .

'Although no wine is made in the country no less nor worse wine is drunk for that reason. The delicacy of the in-habitants' palate is great in this & many other matters. They spare nothing to have the best wines of France. Bordeaux, Bayonne & the other renowned Vineyards keep them in stock; as long as they are the best, the price is not a con-sideration, & it is not spared . . .

'Among the richer inhabitants the wines of the Canaries, Madeira, all sort of liqueurs & the best brandies of Europe are to be found. The English bring bottled beer, cider and all the liqueurs that their country & surrounding countries produce, to the great profit of Medicine & to the detriment of health.'

In 1762 the French government made a bid to achieve not riches but power using this supposed paradise. Paris had just lost the Seven Years' War and had had to surrender half the islands of the Caribbean to the British. Choiseul, Louis XV's minister, decided that a new colony must be founded where a sturdy population of native-born Frenchmen would build a safe base for a new French fleet which one day, sooner or later, would take vengeance on Perfidious Albion. Kourou was chosen as the spot. On 20 December 1763 eight vessels – *Normandie, Danube, La Fortune, Navette, L'Aimable Thérèse, Jupiter, Gloire* and *Saint-Philippe* – reached Guyane with the first colonists for Choiseul's great enterprise. Some of them, thinking of Canada, brought woolly caps and ice skates. In all 16,446 came. Within a few years the survivors, no more than 6,000, had to be shipped home.

France never did recover its empire in America.

The optimists in Paris nevertheless never gave up their efforts at lobbying for a big national effort to open up Guyane. In 1943 when the Second World War was at its height the Académie des Sciences Coloniales reported the lecture of M Blaringhem, Professor at the Sorbonne, on the subject of the future of French Guiana.

'Cayenne,' he enthused, 'will be the Paris of America, the Monaco of the Atlantic. The future is the colonies', let us not dwell on the present; it is the future we have to prepare. French Guiana is almost the only country which enjoys that privileged position of being thrust into the Ocean, within range of Africa and Europe, almost the same distance from New York. It will never be a great country. It will always be a little staging post in those great expeditions where French intelligence and will can impose their tastes and, I hope, their successes on countries which will avail themselves of them, now Equatorial Africa, now North America, now South America and above all tropical South-East America. At the moment about a quarter of South America is given over to European crops: wheat, barley etc and to stockrearing: sheep, horses and other things which are the extensions of European success. But three-quarters of South America is unexplored or unused . . .'

His vision of the future of the colony knew no bounds. Steel could be made with local ores smelted by the charcoal made from the coconuts of the magnificent local palm trees. Such was the plethora of varieties of plant life that the territory could become a nursery for the whole world . . . Projects came tumbling from the good professor's lips like so much tropical rain. On one subject at least he returned to the realm of reality. The key, he said, to attracting the good European labouring stock to the country which was needed to exploit these riches was to get rid of *le bagne*.

Blaringhem's dream went the same way as Choiseul's. Perhaps this time it will do better.

Max Hauzard, a stocky bespectacled Belgian from Liège, has been at Kourou for eight years. He is a senior official with a large bungalow overlooking the sea. A Francophile who plans to retire soon to France, he thinks that Kourou must and will succeed.

'It's a wonderful place if you like sport and nature. When I was younger I liked to go out hunting. I once bagged a tapir. The other day I pulled a fish out of the river that big.' His arms extend. 'One got away. It nearly pulled me in. It was that size.' And his arms extend a little wider.

Hauzard says Kourou is not what it was when he first arrived. 'They're building the houses too close together these days,' he complains. 'In the beginning they gave us more space.'

Spacious or not, Kourou is expanding fast. Not far away is the barracks of the Foreign Legion, on its gates the motto *Legio Patria Mea* – The Legion is my Fatherland. Up the river they are building a dam so the town and the rocket site will have their own power. The main road which passes within a mile of the launch site is being rerouted for security purposes eight miles away. This time Kourou is being protected not evacuated.

Westward along Route Nationale 1 the road gets worse. Long potholed stretches alternate with awkward bridges over rivers like the Sinamary, the Iracoubo or the Mana, each of which rivals in volume the Seine, the Rhône or the Loire. On either side palms offer their coconuts for the traveller's refreshment – if, that is, he can survive the mosquitoes that attack every animate thing that wanders off the road. Here and there are the market garden settlements of the Hmongs, peasant people who lived under French rule in Vietnam and who have travelled across the world to provide some of the labour that Guyane needs.

After cutting through some dense jungle RN1 finally peters out at Saint-Laurent beside the majestic Maroni. Saint-Laurent itself is a nondescript little town, but one where the spirit of the penal colony, of which it was the administrative centre, is still alive.

The biggest building is the old prison hospital, a peeling white multi-storeyed wooden construction in its own grounds which was put up to succour the *bagnards*, the convicts, who died like flies. It stands on the main thoroughfare, again Avenue Charles de Gaulle. (For a territory which was loyally pro-Vichy during the Second World War this latter-day attachment to the leader of the Free French has its ironies.)

Along the avenue, as befits the second town of a French *département* stand its *mairie* and its *sous-prefecture*. There are two hotels, Le Toucan and The Star, a cinema and a video shop, a Vietnamese restaurant, a scrubby football pitch and a large cemetery, and a string of Chinese-owned supermarkets.

But it is at the riverside that Saint-Laurent comes alive. A quay with a little stone jetty sticking into the muddy foreshore is the real *raison d'être* of the town. By the quay lie a score of massive canoes, eighty feet long or more, each hollowed out of some hardwood giant of the forest, equipped with a powerful outboard motor and capable of carrying tons of cargo up the Maroni, the river that the Dutch know as the Marowijne, over the rapids and into the remote heartlands of Guyane and Surinam. Into these smooth, elegant and highly efficient craft are packed drums of oil, bags of rice, passengers, consignments of cigarettes and rum, babies, anything and anyone that needs to get to the hinterland.

To the quay comes the produce of the interior, fruit and coconuts and, well packaged and protected, the gold yielded up by the river. There has always been a golden strand in Guyane's history. This region had also tempted Sir Walter Raleigh and other lesser adventurers to come exploring for El Dorado. No one was in any doubt that the rivers, if tackled skilfully, could be made to give up their gold. One Indian chief was reported to wear round his neck a nugget weighing three or four pounds.

The first gold rush came in 1855 when a good deal was found on the upper reaches of the Approuage River. Gold fever spread to Paris where Guyane was seen as France's Australia and California rolled into one. The Compagnie Aurifère et Agricole de l'Approuage was formed and 4,000 shares of 100 francs were sold out in a few hours. It did not live up to expectations.

There was another gold rush more than thirty years later, on the Awa River. France and Holland were both claiming the area round the headquarters of the Maroni. But Tsar Alexander III, the mediator, judged in favour of Holland and another dream of riches for Guyane was destroyed. A few prospectors did make their fortunes on the Awa; the records speak of the lucky ones carrying away sixty kilos of the metal. As in other gold fields the best money was probably made by the merchants. After all a kilo of rice cost 4 grammes of gold, a kilo of salt cod, 8 grammes, a kilo of sugar, 10 grammes and a litre of wine brought across the Atlantic and paddled 200 miles up river from Saint-Laurent, 15 grammes.

Just upstream are the rusting remains of a gold dredger long since abandoned by some failed mining company. The package tourists who trickle into Guyane and who want to be shepherded into a night in the jungle may for a few francs more go panning for gold. But, lest Monsieur and Madame Dupont have dreams of overnight tropical riches, the cautious brochure primly adds, 'The finding of gold is not guaranteed'.

Brown like all Guyane's rivers, and miles wide, the Maroni is the frontier with Surinam. Across the river on the horizon is Albina, the Surinamese town, recently the victim of the civil war between Colonel Desi Bouterse, the dictator, and the conservative rebels, led by Ronny Brunswijk. Big armed patrol launches of the Gendarmerie Nationale still lie in the river like crocodiles ready to intercept any Surinamese intruder into French waters.

'The Maroni is not so much a frontier as a great boulevard,' says Artigalas.

Two months of the year are given over to carnival in Guyane. Carnival is a thing to be savoured and enjoyed over the weeks rather than guzzled down over a few days as the neighbouring Brazilians do in Rio de Janeiro and Bahia. Every Sunday for eight weeks the avenue Charles de Gaulle in Cayenne is given over to the ragged, high-spirited crowds of revellers. Some come in groups dressed up, say, as Spanish penitents in pointed cowls or decked out with electric light bulbs as the spirit of electricity.

Many, white and black, just arrive, with a drum, a trombone or a trumpet, a François Mitterrand mask or a gorilla's head, ready to throw flour at the onlookers, pinch pretty girls' bottoms or fart, belch and generally gesticulate at the *bons bourgeois*.

On the pavements in their little vans the sellers of chips, cold beer and soft drinks sweat over their portable gas rings and ice boxes and are glad.

But the real spirit of collective joy does not come till just before nightfall when the Haïtians arrive. The big notice on the truck proclaims *'Bossa Combo d'Haïti'* and the amplifiers over the cab take up and magnify a thousandfold the rhythms of the musicians aboard. A wave of ecstatic Haïtians jogs in time up the street sweeping everyone and everything aside, leaving us whites beached like so much tired flotsam at the edge of the crowd. The unalloyed, communal rejoicing of the Haïtians, the nearest thing you get in Guyane today to the black slaves of old, brings back the authentic feeling of the first West Indian carnivals, before the time of canned beer, chips or rubber masks.

But by sundown on Sunday one rite of Guyanese carnival has already been officiated. The chatty matron at the car hire office first told me about it on the day I arrived.

'I shall look out for you tonight at Chez Nana,' she said. 'It's no good getting there before one o'clock in the morning.'

Luc's secretary took up the intrigue later. 'Late on Saturday night everyone goes to Chez Nana,' she said. 'The women go completely disguised. We are the *touloulous*, masked, in long dresses, long sleeves and long gloves. So you can't tell even if we're black or white. We invite the men to dance. It makes a change from being wallflowers waiting for someone to dance with you. Chez Nana is a very special place. It's used only at carnival time. The rest of the year it's deserted.'

She added, rather patronizingly, I thought, 'It allows the men to get rid of the excess nervous energy they store up over the winter. You can't pretend the men put much energy into their jobs here in Guyane.'

Chez Nana or Au Soleil Levant, the Rising Sun, to give it its formal name, is an unprepossessing dance hall on the edge of town. Just after midnight it was clear that Luc's secretary had been right. The road outside was a mass of men, women, cars, taxis and vans selling beer and snacks.

The *touloulous* were there in full force, totally, enigmatically anonymous behind masks which went from elegant Venetian contraptions of velvet and lace to plastic likenesses of Marie-Antoinette or Marilyn Monroe. Inside under a corrugated roof a dozen (male) musicians, white and black, beat out dizzying rhythms to a mass of heaving, shuffling dancers. It was an incomparable blend of *Così fan Tutte* and tropical ardour.

'I'm Luc's secretary,' said a muffled figure and we danced.

'Yes,' I said.

I shall go back to Chez Nana one day. Before I'm too old.

Author's Note

I would like to acknowledge with thanks the help friends in Britain and the Caribbean have given me in my attempts to understand the Caribbean. Foremost among them are Dr Pamela Beschoff, Anne Braithwaite, Professor Alistair Hennessy and Rickey Singh. The views I express here are of course my own.

Thanks, too, to Donald Trelford, the editor of the *Observer*, who provided me with many opportunities to travel to the region, Euan Cameron at Century, and to my agent, Gill Coleridge and her assistant, Clare Roberts.